The Children's War

RUTH INGLIS

The Children's War

Evacuation 1939–1945

COLLINS
8 Grafton Street, London W1
1989

William Collins Sons & Co. Ltd
London · Glasgow · Sydney · Auckland
Toronto · Johannesburg

BRITISH LIBRARY CATALOGUING IN PUBLICATION DATA

Inglis, Ruth
Evacuation: the children's war.
1. Great Britain. Children. Evacuation, 1939–1945.
I. Title.
940.53'151'0941

ISBN 0-00-217710-2

First published 1989
Copyright © Ruth Inglis 1989

Photoset in Linotron Baskerville by
Rowland Phototypesetting Ltd
Bury St Edmunds, Suffolk
Made and printed in Great Britain by
William Collins Sons & Co. Ltd, Glasgow

To my darling MAISIE

Contents

Illustrations

Acknowledgements

When writing a social history, it's the libraries you need, and the kindness of librarians. I found this in abundance, from the librarians at the Boston Public Library newspaper archives who even helped me place stubborn spools into micro-film viewers to the endlessly patient Dorothy Sheridan and her colleague, Victoria Allanson, Sussex University Mass Observation Archive, who do not seem to mind unearthing quantities of old wartime letters for one's perusal.

An unexpected treasure discovered in the course of my research was my local East End library in Lea Bridge Road, Leyton, rather grandly called the Carnegie Library in spite of its humble turn-of-the-century rococo exterior, and possessing one of the most extensive collections of World War II books I've come across anywhere. The London Library's selection of 1940s literature was invaluable, as was its generosity in allowing me to keep reference books out for so long.

Then there were the journalists. Where did they get the reputation for being competitive with their fellows? Peter Lewis, author of *A People's War*, and Ralph Barker, who wrote *Children of the Benares*, the recent exposé of the sinking of the evacuee ship, were exceedingly generous with both permission to quote from their books and with the names of evacuees to interview.

I shall bid a small, sad goodbye and thanks to my brave 'trekker' friend Betty Pooley, who always encouraged me to write this book and tell her story. She died in 1987, alas, at the age of seventy-seven, but not before living a full life, bringing up her two boys in wartime and working tirelessly as a postal clerk at the *Daily Express*. It sounded as if she had had a rough war but she roared with laughter as she recounted it, apparently thinking most of it hilarious. Her mirth reminded me of what I once heard described as 'Chinese laughter' – fatalistic and a little black (I have always thought the

British and Chinese alike in their sense of humour and maybe that's why, having grown up in Manchuria, I feel at home here). Betty's laughter got her through some bad times, as it did, I believe, many other evacuees and their long-suffering parents.

My appreciation goes to Bill Irving, Deputy Headmaster of Chesterton County Primary School, Cirencester, for inviting me to his school to see a video of the re-enactment of Evacuation Day, 1 September 1939. Sixty primary school children spent a day caught in a time warp playing the roles of evacuees, complete with lunchboxes, name tags and gas masks on 25 April 1986. Caught up in the excitement of living history, the children I spoke to at Chesterton – ten year olds mostly – felt proud of those long-ago warriors. And so they should be. It *was* a children's war.

Warm thanks to my dear friend Betty Allsop, who was both encouraging and knowledgeable about the war. I am thankful, too, for the help extended by my Pine Manor College mate and fellow alumna, Anne Bortraeger Orser, who helped me find two English evacuees who were sent to America with long-lasting results.

Gratitude goes to Christopher Dowling and Anita Ballin of the Imperial War Museum who steered me in the direction of some helpful local historians. It was through them, too, that I met Dame Josephine Barnes, who has given me many useful insights into those troubled war years in which she played a vital part.

Thanks to all my evacuee interviewees who let me badger them for their memories, some of which they had repressed, they said. Many confessed that the exercise in memory excavation had been therapeutic. I hope so. And I am grateful to Hilary Granger of Woodbridge, Suffolk, who let me borrow her charming small girl's evacuee diary ('the vicar told us that war had been declared . . . and we had sausages for dinner . . .').

My gratitude also goes to Toni Woollcott, superlative typist and young mother; this manuscript grew with her second baby, now nearly due. By a lucky chance her mother, Kathy Tuffin, was an evacuee and her memories of being sent to a Lancashire mill town from London at the age of eight are among the most evocative in the book.

And of course, love to my grown-up children, Diana and Neil, who have been continuous, first-hand contacts with the way that growing children think and sift experience. And to Eric, who suffered the pounding of my tinny, worn-out portable through some chilly East Anglian months, and remained consistently supportive, as always.

Government evacuation scheme 1939–45

Based on local counts of evacuees taken generally at six-monthly intervals throughout the war.

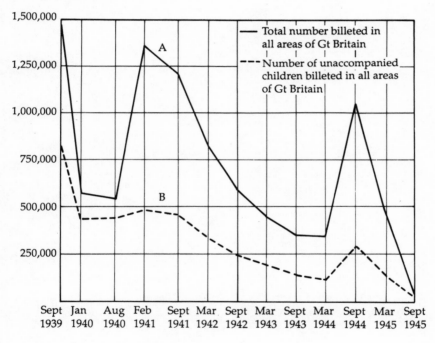

From R. M. Titmuss's '*Problems of Social Policy*', in *Official History of the Second World War*, p. 356.

1

E-Day: The First Exodus

Much has been said about D-Day and the Normandy Landings but little has been written in recent years about that other extraordinary day – E-Day, as it could be called: Evacuation Day – 1 September 1939. Scores of mothers and children, and teachers with large parties of schoolchildren, were sent almost blindly into the British countryside to ensure their safety in the event of a bombing attack on the cities (which was feared to be imminent). It was also called the 'Phoney War Evacuation' because bombs did not, in fact, drop for a further eleven months after it took place. 1,473,500 people left the cities for rural billets in Great Britain under official aegis, among them 99,000 mothers and children, and 62,000 children in school parties. Pregnant women, the blind, and the homeless combined to make up the total figure of almost one and a half million people.

There were to be two other large British evacuation movements during the five years and eight months of the war. The Second Evacuation, organized by the government, began in August 1940, with the onset of the Battle of Britain, when approximately 1,250,000 women and children were assigned to rural billets (141,000 of the total number were unaccompanied children). The exodus took place in the most savage period of the Blitz – the autumn of 1940 – and was a very real life-saver, making the false alert of the Phoney War Evacuation of 1939 seem, in retrospect, an excellent practice run.

The final and Third Evacuation came in 1944 with the 'flying bombs' scare. Doodlebugs were pilotless planes which appeared in mid-June 1944, and provoked the flight of over a million people, largely escaping from London and its suburbs; 101,000 unac-companied children and 183,000 mothers and children were involved (invalids, the elderly, pregnant women, and hospital and nursery inmates made up the total number). The flying

bombs period stretched over ten months: initially only V-1
missiles were dropped; the even more destructive and larger
rockets, called V-2s, were used together with the V-1s to spread
terror throughout the final months of the war. Such attacks only
ceased in March 1945.

While these are the officially recorded numbers involved in the
three major evacuation movements, the figures represent merely a
rough guide because of the continuous shiftings of evacuees and
their mothers, or evacuees on their own. They would return home
when the bombs weren't dropping; flee again in droves from the
cities when they were.

Helping to muddy the statistical waters were privately organized
evacuations; the spontaneous 'trekking' from southern coastal
towns, and from Liverpool, London, Manchester and other centres
when the bombing became intolerable and the shelters stuffy and
squalid from overcrowding. Such spontaneous evacuations were
usually aided, in part, by the state.

Also confusing the totals involved in the evacuations were the
more general and expensive private arrangements made by the
middle-classes, which went unrecorded but were believed to add
up to two million people over the war period.

And then, of course, there were overseas evacuations in 1940 and
1941, when children embarked from the ports of Southampton and
Liverpool to safety in North America, South Africa, New Zealand
and Australia. Five thousand women and children travelled overseas under government supervision. Privately organized groups
were not officially tabulated and therefore no exact figures exist for
this self-styled evacuation either.

I will concentrate, for the most part, in the pages that follow, on
the evacuations that took place in England and Wales, because
although Scotland witnessed population movements of corresponding interest – and Clydeside and other Scottish cities were equally
ravaged by bombs – the Scottish evacuation was organized autono-
mously. Scottish children did not go off to 'destinations unknown',
in school parties, as they did in other parts of the UK.

For someone like myself, intrigued by the personal impact of
evacuation, interest centres on those young children over the age
of five, who were uprooted from their homes and separated from
their parents, and who headed out in school parties for the country-

side in trains and buses. How did the boys and girls react? What did the parents feel as they waved their children goodbye?

I have spent several years trying to find out, both by delving into some as yet unpublished material at the Mass Observation* Archives at Sussex University and by interviewing the grown-up graduates of the experience, now in their late middle age. I have come to the conclusion that there are almost as many reactions to their long-ago uprooting as there were evacuees, but one common thread uniting them is that the experience was rarely considered sinister in retrospect, though some wrenching homesickness and antipathy to foster-parents was felt at the time.

The first, Phoney War Evacuation was indeed an almost light-hearted affair. One thoughtful evacuee told me that she always contrasted it in her mind with other newsreel footage she had seen, showing Jewish people herded into trains, the dreadful Final Solution, which began two years later – 1941 – in Europe. She commented:

> The twentieth century is as much about cramming people into trains as about bombs though the atmosphere of our evacuation was extraordinarily light-hearted considering the adult fears that had made it come to pass. Certainly, some of us suffered from full bladders and hunger, a little discomfort perhaps, but by and large it was viewed as a rather larky business altogether.

With boxed gas masks and brown paper parcels of clothes and food dangling from their arms and from around their necks, name tags tied to their sleeves and lapels, unaccompanied older children, and mothers shepherding their under-fives poured onto the station platforms of the teeming and often slum-ridden cities of Britain.

The enthusiasm with which the population embraced the First Evacuation was exceedingly varied. The northern exodus of school-children was particularly successful: nearly three-quarters of the

---

*Mass Observation: this team of investigators into public opinion, which started in Bolton and Blackpool, Lancs. in 1937, led by Tom Harrisson, was made up of students, artists, writers, photographers and local people. MO regularly produced typewritten reports which summarized information culled from observations, descriptions and overheard conversations. During the years of war, the MO team provided the Home Intelligence Department with material about wartime civilian morale. Its compelling findings are to be found in 'files' and diaries in the Mass Observation Archives in the University of Sussex library.

child population of Manchester, Newcastle, Liverpool, Bootle
and other Merseyside districts crowded into the trains. London
saw a fairly brisk response to the government's plea to leave, with
nearly half the children going. For some reason – probably
parental reluctance to be parted from their children – only a
quarter of the children in the towns in the West Midlands were
evacuated.

Among the better off, private evacuation had been going on at a
furious rate throughout the summer of 1939 although, as Richard
Titmuss complained in his official history of World War II, it was
impossible to make an accurate estimate of the extent of it. Besides
mothers and children, those also listed in the government evacuation
scheme, he reports, included 'homeless persons, expectant mothers,
children in nurseries, camps and hostels, old people, the crippled,
the blind, civil defence personnel and emergency medical staff'.
The 13,000 expectant mothers who departed their homes is one
particularly evocative statistic he quotes. Miraculously, not one
person was hurt in this gigantic, confused and somewhat bumbling
operation, a triumph of the much-maligned British capacity to
'muddle through'.

Not that there had been anything fly-by-night in the government's
advance planning for E-Day. The planners had started organizing
the exodus as long ago as 1934. (An evacuation sub-committee
report was published in secret that year: the need for an evacuation
from London was never questioned.) In April 1935 anti-gas precautions for children and adults were being discussed and three
years later, in May 1938, the London County Council passed a
resolution approving the principle of evacuating schoolchildren.
Some wavering occurred about whether evacuation should be compulsory or voluntary; this argument was resolved in July 1938 when
a report was issued stating that evacuation should be voluntary.
This policy had far-reaching and not always happy results, as it left
parents with the critical decision about whether to keep their
children with them, where they would be loved and cared for, or to
send them away, where they would be safer but might not be as
happy as they would be at home.

In spite of all this prior planning, the E-Day Evacuation was
fairly raggedly carried out and a cynic might say that it didn't
deserve to succeed as well as it did. Since the German bombers did

not appear over Britain in earnest until the spring of 1940, and two-thirds of the evacuated population had returned to their homes by January 1940, it could be considered a farce.

But was it? Many historians such as Titmuss think not; it acted as a perfect practice run for the two subsequent evacuations which *were* necessary when the Germans blitzed the major cities. Only 7736 children were killed in bomb attacks in the UK throughout the entire course of the war and unquestionably this figure would have been much higher had there been no evacuation policy established from the beginning. Decanting children from the cities into rural billets was an admirable idea, but it is also true that the First Evacuation in September 1939 was premature.

Looking back over the war years, one could be forgiven for believing almost superstitiously that September was a fateful month for Britain. One year before the Phoney War Evacuation of 1 September 1939, on 30 September 1938, Prime Minister Neville Chamberlain had been foolishly traduced by Hitler at Munich. Chamberlain returned to London the next day, waving a fluttering bit of paper which, he said, proved that Germany had renounced its war-like intentions. He heralded what he described as 'peace for our time'. A year later the deluded and crestfallen Chamberlain was obliged to declare war on Germany. In a broadcast from Downing Street at 11:15 a.m. on Sunday, 3 September 1939, he announced:

> This morning the British Ambassador in Berlin handed the German Government a final Note stating that unless he heard from them by eleven o'clock that they were prepared at once to withdraw their troops from Poland a state of war would exist between us.

A little more than a year later, on 15 September 1940, the RAF's 'Few'* gained the upper hand in the Battle of Britain. It was then that the German Luftwaffe, with 3500 aircraft positioned in the

---

*The Few, taken from Winston Churchill's speech: 'Never in the field of human conflict was so much owed by so many to so few.' The 'few' were the 2949 RAF pilots and aircrew who fought in the sixty-six operational fighter squadrons from 10 July to 31 October 1940, the precise dates of the Battle of Britain, Churchill's name for this harrowing, defensive battle in which the British only had 700 serviceable planes – compared to the Luftwaffe's 3500 – two-thirds Hurricanes, most of the rest Spitfires.

defeated Low Countries, France and Norway, realized that England could not be defeated in the air: sixty German aircraft were destroyed on that day as against twenty-five British fighter planes. The German High Command put aside its invasion plans. For three successive years September was, therefore, a crucial month for the British people.

However, in the autumn of 1939, when the war was still considered a 'Bore War', the most potent emotion most parents felt when considering the outcome of the First Evacuation was extreme irritation. What had it all been about they wondered, and why had they been forced to endure both a painful separation from their children and the heavy expenditure of billeting costs (8s 6d or 42p a week for a child under 16)? The most serious consequence of the First (apparently meaningless) Evacuation, was to make parents weary of the to'ings and fro'ings they had endured, and somewhat blasé when confronted a year later with the Second Evacuation which *was* necessary. Government posters imploring parents to evacuate their children to the country began to appear in force again in the winter of 1940. Such a massive propaganda drive underscored parental ennui with the scheme and exposed what a psychological (if not practical) blunder the initial evacuation had been.

What prompted the normally low-key, unhysterical British government and public to overreact so dramatically on 1 September 1939? Why did so many instantly flee to the countryside? The answer was that the British people and its leaders felt a desperate sense of unpreparedness in the face of mounting German aggression. Winston Churchill noted, in the first volume of his war memoirs, *The Gathering Storm*, that in 1935:

> A disaster of first magnitude had fallen upon us. Hitler had already obtained parity with Great Britain. Henceforward he had merely to drive his factories and training-schools at full speed not only to keep his lead in the air, but steadily to improve it. Henceforward all the unknown, immeasurable threats which overhung London from air attack would be a definite and compelling factor in all our decisions. However, we could never catch up; or at any rate the Government never did catch up.

The conviction that Germany was mighty and well-armed while Britain was weak and unprepared helped fuel substantial panic in the nation during the years leading up to the formal declaration of war by Chamberlain on 3 September 1939. Fears which were well founded (of bomb blitzes that would become a horrific reality by September 1940) flowered side by side with fears which were groundless. Some believed the German hordes would try to invade island Britain by sending, in advance, large numbers of parachutists.

It was also thought the Germans would use poison gas; for this reason 38 million gas masks were issued to adults and children alike in 1938. (The masks were too big to be worn by infants so none were issued for the under-twos; however, an incubator-like canister and 'Mickey Mouse' masks were subsequently developed to protect babies and young children.) One abiding image of the First Evacuation was of children carrying gas masks but not much else (rarely even a change of clothes and with only a meagre sandwich, a bit of chocolate and perhaps an apple in their lunch boxes) marching to stations.

For the children, the expedition to the railway stations had a festive air. As TV presenter Michael Aspel, now in his mid-fifties, recalls in his amiable memoir quoted in the book *The Evacuees*:

Somebody remarked afterwards that it was as if the Pied Piper had come back. The scene had changed from Hamelin to South London, and the River Weser, deep and wide, was now the Wandle, which was narrow and smelled.

But it was a bright, clear day, a good day for travelling. We marched through the streets of Wandsworth, just as we'd done before, with labels round our necks, heading for the railway station. Only this time people stood on their doorsteps to watch us pass, the shopkeepers gave us sweets and packets of nuts and raisins. And this time, instead of assembling on the platform at Earlsfield station then marching back to school again, they put us on a train. Of course it was all a game to us . . . I have a picture in my mind of the steps of Earlsfield station. There are short legs by the score, clambering upwards, none shorter or fatter than my brother Alan's. He was four years old and surprisingly delicate for such a chubby little boy. The steps he was climbing were only a few hundred yards from our street, but he didn't see it again for another five years.

Fat legs and floppy name labels! Both conjure up a vivid and somewhat pathetic picture, but the presence of gas masks around the children's necks adds a grim note. It had been drilled into them that they had to wear their gas masks, either on their faces or on their bodies, at all hours of the day – even in bed.

There was also a prevailing fear of burns: when mothers and school-teachers remembered, the children also carried anti-burn cream as one grown-up evacuee recounted to author Norman Longmate. A Hornsey schoolboy of nine at the time, he remembers exactly what he had to carry because it was so heavy:

I paraded with the other children from Tollington School outside Hornsey station as heavily loaded as a soldier in full marching kit. A gas mask in a white tin box stuffed with sticky plaster, anti-burn cream and iodine pulled me down on one side; a haversack crammed with sandwiches and apples balanced me on the other. Brown paper parcels hung from my belt like grenades – emergency sandwiches, spare socks if my feet got wet, a mackintosh cape, a slab of chocolate. In my pocket were labels, displaying my school, home address and destination; in one hand I carried a brown suitcase containing clothes, in the other a wad of comics.

This Hornsey lad must have come from a middle-class home judging from the magnificence of his rations and his large stock of clothes.

One of the most profound effects of the evacuation was to bring to the nation's attention the shocking disparity in child care in Britain and the extremes of wealth and poverty that divided the country. Many slum children arrived at the reception centres kitted out with no more than what they stood in and what they stood in was modest enough. (Liverpool urchins were dubbed the kids from 'Plimsoll City' because of their footwear, shoes totally inadequate for rural winters and icy country mud. For the first time, the evacuation experience exposed class delineations as effectively as a felled tree trunk exposes the tree's growth.)

The evidence of class divisions was an uncomfortable and unexpected side-effect of the mass exodus of 1939. It caused Vera Brittain, a sensitive chronicler of the times, to exclaim that 'the evacuation scheme exposed the sorrowful truth that one half of England did not know how the other half lived'.* Others held the

*See Chapter 2, p.34 and Chapter 5, pp. 85–8.

same conviction, leading many of them to suggest in the years to come that this migration, revealing deprivation as it did, laid the foundations of the Welfare State. But although these shocked ruminations were to be echoed later on in the war by government planners themselves, at first officialdom was primarily obsessed with the population's physical safety.

From the moment war was declared, it was believed that bombs would rain down on the big cities. Anderson shelters were dug in back gardens (the dug-outs were named after Sir John Anderson, then Lord Privy Seal) and a strict blackout was enforced. In the Phoney War period this latter precaution caused more deaths than any anticipated enemy action; more than 4000 people were killed on the roads late in 1939 – double the usual figure – a direct result of the murk that engulfed the towns and country roads (headlamps were blacked out, too, with cloth and cardboard covers).

According to Peter Lewis, author of *A People's War*, the government expected there would be 'fifty casualties per ton of bombs unloaded on London, for example, in the first fourteen days of the war'. These calculations, he says, were based on figures relating to World War 1 and were scary enough to make people accept black-outs, air raid precautions, rude wardens, automobile accidents and pedestrian casualties as unavoidable facts of life.

The formation of the Local Defence Volunteers, the LDV (later to be known as the Home Guard) provides a graphic illustration of the anxiety at work in a frustrated populace that knew a war was on – but just *where* was it? The underlying fear had produced the premature evacuation of the children from the cities on 1 September; the non-events of the Phoney War which followed, dragging on from Chamberlain's declaration of war in September 1939 well into the late spring of 1940, gave time for panic to flourish, and last-minute – often comically conceived – preparations for open warfare to be made.

The LDV was established on 14 May 1940 by Anthony Eden who, as Secretary of State for War, invited all men to 'supplement resources as yet untapped'. He went on to exhort millions of male radio listeners to heights of patriotic fervour by announcing:

> . . . You will not be paid, but you will receive uniform and will be armed. In order to volunteer, what you have to do is to give

in your names at your local police station and then, as and when we want you, we will let you know . . .

Charles Graves, historian of this bizarre movement and himself an LDV stationed in Sussex, writes in *The Home Guard of Britain* that 'thousands of men arrived at police stations (to volunteer) while the broadcast was still in progress'. There were 10,000 volunteers from Kent alone in the first twenty-four hours. Whether this was fervour or just plain fever the British population was truly in ferment.

The volunteers weren't to know that German parachutists would rarely appear in the skies over Britain except when trying to escape from burning planes. However, the background against which the LDV was formed was desperate enough. As Graves comments:

On May 13th, Holland was swarming with parachute troops, the Maginot Line had been dented in two places, the Ardennes had been penetrated . . . It was now apparent that the whole structure of the Allied defence on the Continent was collapsing rapidly.

It was against this mid-May background of collapse and conflagration that the eloquent and charismatic new Prime Minister, Winston Churchill,* made his ringing inaugural speech to the House of Commons on 13 May, calling for the nation to 'wage war by sea, land and air; war with all our might and with all the strength that God can give us'.

The LDV took up his invitation almost literally, especially about waging war by land. Anthony Eden also stoked the warlike enthusiasm of the volunteers by describing the parachute manoeuvres the Germans had been employing so successfully against Holland and Belgium. He explained that their purpose was 'to disorganize and confuse as a preparation for the landing of troops by aircraft'. On the same day the BBC announced in its German news that any German parachutist found landing in Britain in any kit other than a recognized German uniform would be instantly shot.

The Home Guard became increasingly haunted by the spectre of a sky full of German parachutists, many of them in mufti, preparing the way for a massive and instantaneous invasion of troops. Shoot first, ask questions later, they were told – only shooting wasn't so

---

*Prime Minister Neville Chamberlain had resigned on 10 May in response to the shocking news of the German invasion of the Low Countries.

easy. Hardly any of the volunteers had ever handled a gun to do anything more serious than take a pot shot at a rabbit. (Ironically, as many will recall, rabbits loomed symbolically large in the public psyche in the early part of the war. The music hall song 'Run, Rabbit, Run' captured the battle cry of a nation determined to have Hitler 'on the run' in no time.)

Charles Graves goes on to describe what happened when he and his Home Guard colleagues in Sussex (a body of men composed of vets, butchers and farmers from the surrounding villages) tired of keeping vigil on the sleepy Downs from dusk to dawn for parachutists who didn't appear:

> We raked over the whole district for firearms . . . We built up an armoury at first in one of the upper rooms at the pub. We heard that a very patriotic woman in the village had some shooting irons, so we called to see her. One of the walls of her cottage was decorated with guns of all ages and sizes. They had been her late husband's treasures. She willingly lent us two, but she declined to let us take a natty little revolver. 'I am keeping that myself for the first German who sets foot in this village,' she said. One of our squad said his farmer boss had a lovely shotgun he had always envied . . . We went to try and get it, but had no luck. Eventually we were sent eight Ross rifles, and with these and four shotguns and one revolver we made a brave show in our first real parade one Sunday morning in a field behind the pub. We spent some more of our funds buying ammunition for the shotguns.

The fumblings of the LDV, bravely wresting guns from widows for hand-to-hand battles with non-existent enemies, amuse us now. But their anxiety was real enough and some of their worst fears did eventually materialize in the autumn of 1940 and thereafter when the German blitzkrieg produced more fire, death and chaos in the cities than even the most willing platoon of firefighters and fire wardens could handle. When nemesis did arrive in the form of tons of blitzkrieg bombs, it was not a case of fears being realized, however, so much as of their being different. The Home Guard had had hand-to-hand combat in mind rather than the faceless, night-by-night destruction of aerial bombardment.

*

Thoughtful Britons in the late 1930s had had to try to piece together
what would happen in case of war from memories of a devastating
past world conflict and from the skewed predictions of Whitehall
bureaucrats. Above all, an abiding belief that the children should
be saved, at all costs, underscored much of the thinking in 1938
and 1939 and was the reason tens of thousands of them were sent
into the rural areas on that famous September day in 1939. If their
journey proved unnecessary first time round, the reasoning behind
it *was* sound nonetheless, and the child-centred concern totally
laudable.

There was a tender 'suffer the children' protectiveness at work in
the British adult psyche in the late 30s which revealed itself both
in government dicta and in the workings of private charities engaged
in the machinery of evacuation. At the launching of one of the first
evacuations of children by sea, on the *Batory*,* which took 477
children to Sydney, Australia, in October 1940, an official actually
voiced the public's sentiment: 'We're asking you to take the Crown
Jewels.'

That the planning preceding the massive E-Day migration was
entirely inadequate to the tender feelings which motivated it was
also true. According to Richard Titmuss:

> When the order for evacuation was given by the Cabinet on
> 31st August there were, in the reception areas, no reception
> hostels or sick bays; maternity accommodation was quite inad-
> equate in most places; none of the camps was ready; beds,
> blankets, crockery, black-out material, furniture, lighting, heat-
> ing, cooking and many kinds of equipment and categories of
> staff were either insufficient or in the wrong places. Moreover,
> as was only to be expected, the standard – in quantity and
> quality – of the social services in the rural areas was inferior
> to that in London and other big cities. Even so, there was
> at least one county authority which proceeded to curtail its
> maternity and child welfare activities in the belief that such
> things were unnecessary in wartime.

Titmuss's savage irony is well placed. How could some officials
have thought the war would halt the birth process? But what
angered people even more than such monstrous oversights was the

---

*For further reference to HMS *Batory*, see Chapter 7, p. 114.

slipshod condition of the reception centres designated to accommo-
date the evacuees on arrival. As Titmuss goes on to say:

> Many reports testify to the general confusion and unprepared-
> ness which characterised the reception of the mothers and
> children in September 1939. All the troubles caused by lack of
> pre-knowledge about the evacuees, train delays, the ban on
> spending and other factors, were piled higher when many of
> the parties travelling in crowded trains, sometimes without
> lavatories and adequate water supplies, arrived in a dirty and
> unco-operative state. It was not a good start. Town and country
> met each other in a critical mood.

> The war-time guests of the country were further aggrieved
> when, in many areas, they were walked or paraded around
> while householders took their pick. 'Scenes reminiscent of a
> cross between an early Roman slave market and Selfridge's
> bargain basement ensued.' One boy likened it to 'a cattle
> show', for farmers picked strong-looking lads, and the pre-
> sentable, nicely dressed children were quickly chosen. The
> method of billeting seems generally to have been either direct
> selection by householders or haphazard allotment. Mothers
> were not in demand.

Loaded onto trains and often buses to be transported to
'destinations unknown'* on that long-ago Friday and Saturday
may have seemed like an adventure to the children involved, but
older women roped in as helpers recall the scene differently. My
sister-in-law, Sylvia Woodeson, then in her early twenties, was
asked by her older brother to help him as an evacuation courier
in Bow in the East End. (Their father, a well-to-do steeplejack,
owned one of the grand old houses off the Mile End Road.) She
told me:

> What I recall most vividly were the mothers trying to hold
> back their tears as they marched these little boys and girls in
> their gas masks into the centre where my brother, Sidney, was
> trying to round them up. The children were wild with excite-
> ment but most mums were pale and drawn, no doubt wonder-
> ing when they'd see their sons and daughters again. It was
> certainly the first time the mothers had been parted from their

---

*The secrecy which surrounded the children's destinations, like that which enveloped
troop movements, was thought to be one way of preventing enemy sabotage attempts.

schoolchildren. Very close families were the order of the day in Bow. No one had to tell you about the value of family life in the East End then because, quite frankly, we didn't know anything else.

A young woman courier in Stratford, East London, who had helped her father, a school caretaker, in the same way told Derek Johnson a similar tale of pathetic chaos which he relates in his book, *Exodus of Children*:

> When I arrived home [on Thursday] there were all these little children with their bundles of clothes and gas masks, gathered in the school hall. We hung around all that day and the next but finally, on the Saturday, we were given the word to move out. After all the waiting the poor mites had become very fretful for as what to them had seemed at first a great adventure had now lost all its excitement. We lined the children to check they had everything they had been told to bring and with many tearful farewells marched to Stratford Main Station to wait for the train to take us to some unknown place . . . Eventually, after an awful long wait we were ushered aboard a train and packed into the compartments. There were so many of us crammed aboard it was almost impossible to find room to squat. Of course there were the inevitable tears and some of the kids were sick, and quite a few became very excited when we got into the country, as for many this was the first time they had ever been out of London.

They ended up at Colchester station and were then convoyed in buses and coaches to an old schoolhouse at Little Clacton. For many young East Enders, it was the start of a lifelong love affair with Essex. (It still doesn't seem to occur to the residents of Walthamstow and Leytonstone to head west for Brighton on the weekends.)

To many young teenagers the evacuation was a stimulating and necessary exercise, if they thought seriously about it at all. David Ross, a London journalist and colleague of mine on the *Daily Express* for many years, was fourteen when E-Day arrived. He was a serious Regent Street Polytechnic student whose family lived in Bloomsbury:

> When I was told to get on a train I just believed that that was it – there was no choice. It was assumed London was going to

be razed to the ground. I was convinced of this myself because I was in the Boy Scouts and I had my Civil Defence badge and I thought it might be a good idea to be out of town when this happened. My mother had already gone to the country with my younger brother and sister. I knew nothing about the country but, like my schoolmates, I was fed up and bored about the plans being made to get there. We couldn't tell our parents and it was all secret. Our school party was put on a train for one entire day on 1 September and shunted about, stopping and starting much of the way, finally grinding to a halt near Cheddar Gorge in Somerset. I think the train just ran out of steam. We then went on by coach to Wedmore. I had never seen the countryside before and got a piece of grit in my eye from looking out the train window. I remember the headmaster scolding me for leaning out the window.

For many like Ross, despite the irritations the train trip itself was a marvellous adventure and things like scenery moving outside windows and sudden dips into pitch-black tunnels causes for wonderment. Teachers were there, too, to torment and tease, a source of familiarity linking children with their old lives.

Norah Hodgkin, nearly six at the time of the evacuation, told Derek Johnson that her train trip from Suffolk to Gloucestershire seemed purest mischievous joy; her most vivid memory concerned speeding through the Ipswich railway tunnel in the dark – she had the nerve to get up and poke her middle-aged schoolmistress to frighten her, thus impressing her friends who'd dared her to do so. She was also tickled to see that two of the bigger boys, who had been gorging chocolate and oranges during the trip, came to grief when the taller of them had to use the hood of his friend's coat as a sick bag after all the piggery.

Sickness, weak bladders and consequent puddles, poking teachers, getting grit in the eye, gorging on box lunches, giggles. All this was huge fun. Certainly none of it at this stage seemed the least bit alarming. However, when the children arrived at their reception centres to be billeted, the laughter evaporated like hot air from out of a party balloon.

To repeat Titmuss's resonant, understated phrase: 'Town and country met each other in a critical mood.' That the two should not meld any more easily than the fabled East with West was something that had not entered the minds of those solemn Whitehall planners drafting their blueprints for migration. Certainly they never completely harmonized – but why not?

The 'Phoney' Evacuation: Uneasy Billetings

Much has been said about the clash of urban and rural sensibilities, both in the young and old, which the evacuation brought into sharp relief. Dr Carlton Jackson, an American history professor, puts it very strongly: 'the present day welfare state in Britain owes much of its existence to the evacuation of children during World War II, now nearly half a century ago'. The late Dr Susan Isaacs, writing of the evacuees in Cambridge which she, as a child psychiatrist, observed with a sharp professional, as well as sympathetic feminine eye, remarked that 'Evacuation was proving a powerful social ferment . . .'; 'the country was shocked by the manners and morals of the town'.

The rural foster-parents and citizens comprising the reception committees, who met the children on their village platforms, were not prepared for such filthy children ('found unclean' was the euphemism given by the volunteer workers who greeted them. It could have been a definition of urban poverty, too: head lice were almost unknown in rural areas.) A passion for tabulating percentages was rife in 1939 and one bureaucratic breakdown listed the national infestation ratio – Northern Ireland led the way with 60 per cent. By comparison, South London schoolchildren seemed almost fastidious – just under 20 per cent, or one in five – had lousy heads in Lambeth. Lice-ridden children were treated rather unceremoniously at the station reception centres, often shorn on the spot, without even a nod being given in the direction of obtaining permission first from their parents.

Shocked commentary rumbled through parliament to accompany the news of Britain's lice-ridden population, leading Ernest Brown, the Minister of Health, to exclaim: 'These are not scrofulous and verminous children . . . they are the bud of the nation.' But why was the 'bud of the nation' – plucky, joyous, mischievous train passengers all being trundled to unknown destinations – quite so lousy?

These children from the city slums shocked their frequently prissy hosts because no one, least of all rural voluntary workers and women from such altruistic organizations as the Women's Voluntary Service and the Women's Institute, had been warned, in any realistic way, about their backgrounds. Desperate poverty *was* endemic to the cities, in many cases a legacy of World War I. The parents of the evacuees were themselves World War I babies who had missed routine schooling and regular medical check-ups. Throughout that war, there were never fewer than one-quarter of a million children on poor relief in England and Wales. To quote Richard Titmuss again: 'the pattern of town life exposed during the first evacuation showed the *bills of war* of the past . . . and these were children who couldn't buy safety as two million other people had done'.

Parents who could not afford to pay board and lodgings were not made to do so (see p. 22). They were given 'nil assessment' and their billeting costs were carried by their local councils. Nearly 90 per cent of Scottish mothers and children took advantage of the assisted evacuation schemes in this first evacuation and, though they returned in droves to the cities in January 1940, when the bombs weren't dropping, they again picked up their children and headed for the reception areas in July 1941, when Glasgow and Clydebank began to be blasted (142,000 families from these areas came to the Scottish reception districts at that time). Poverty and the term 'assisted evacuation' became inseparable indicators of economic conditions, particularly in Scotland.

Those who could 'buy safety' did not arrive unceremoniously on station platforms sewn into their clothes, with head lice, and frequently wearing no knickers and no socks. But the poorer evacuees did. They were also the legatees of the Depression, when unemployment was high and household amenities low. Their parents lived in infamous settlements like the Gorbals in Glasgow where the children played with rats and broken glass. For those officials who had time to check their native evacuee population before it departed, the sight was saddening; nearly a fifth were found deficient in footwear and clothing. Most were unscrubbed.

However bleak council tower block flats may appear in Britain's cities today, it is as well to remember that each one has a bathroom and a WC of its own. This was definitely not the case in the late 30s and 40s. In Stepney, East London, for example, 90 per cent of homes were without baths at the war's outset. Insanitary conditions in the 20s arising from World War I were made worse in the 30s by the Depression and undermined every aspect of family life. Britain had one of the highest infant mortality rates in the Western world in the decades leading up to World War II.

As well as fretting at the uncleanliness of the evacuees who poured off the trains and into the reception centres, the volunteers who greeted the children were shocked at their undernourished appearance. The incidence of tubercular children was alarmingly high, and judging from news photographs taken of them on station platforms, they resembled little scarecrows. The volunteer workers publicly voiced their dismay. Soon the nation's nutrition experts were proclaiming that hundreds of thousands of its urban children were living on what began to be called a 'slum diet'.

In a study made by the Hygiene Committee of the Women's Group on Public Welfare and overseen by the Rt Hon. Margaret Bondfield not long after the First Evacuation, the Committee registered its concern. In a section called 'Bad Choice of Food', it reported that 'part of the problem of poverty . . . shows that at the lower income levels diet contains too much starchy food and shows a deficiency in first-class protein and fats and in the protective foods especially green vegetables and fresh fruit.'

Help was speedily provided after the war broke out. Lord Woolton and his Ministry of Food acted with breathtaking alacrity for a large, monolithic ministry; he had the Exchequer financing free or cheap milk in the schools by July 1940, as well as free blackcurrant syrup (later orange juice) and cod liver oil to expectant mothers and all children under five. The Ministry also went into speedy action on the public information front, quite literally making a virtue out of the necessity of food rationing by churning out enlightened nutritional tips to the public about how best to nourish its young. Fish, greens, berry fruit and potatoes in their jackets were among the excellent fibrous and high protein ingredients recommended.

Another strong reason for the shocking condition of the majority of the city children who appeared at the rural reception areas on 1 September 1939 was that they had spent the whole summer running free, playing in the streets, and getting their clothes scruffy. The almost parental supervision of the school authorities in socially conscious cities such as Liverpool, London, Birmingham and Sheffield had been absent for months. School medical inspections had not been carried out on the evacuees for at least three months: a potent cause for their exaggerated condition of medical and physical neglect. All they possessed, it appeared, was their high spirits. It was a tribute to many unprepared foster-parents that this charm and vivacity was enough. Historians of the period bemoaned the propensity of government officials to rely on the innate Christianity and patriotism of its public. In an amazing number of cases, they were not disappointed.

The Ministry of Health struggled manfully to carry out evacuation work, bombs or no bombs, and issued a battery of nannyish, well-meaning memoranda to its billeting officers and voluntary welfare workers. Early in the war Ernest Brown, the Minister of Health, also wrote a rather aggrieved foreword to a pamphlet entitled *Government Evacuation Scheme*, in which he remarked:

> . . . the general public hardly realises how arduous and how important a service is being rendered by this great army of volunteers. The finding of the billet is only the beginning. The real work starts later. Evacuees have to accustom themselves to separation from family and friends, householders to sharing their home with strangers. The process of making a new life together is hard and differences which afterwards seem trifling become magnified by stress of circumstances . . . It is to the Billeting Officer and the local voluntary worker that all these difficulties are brought and it is he, or more often, she who is called on to act as guide, counsellor and friend in matters ranging from the unruly high spirits of small boys to the tracing of lost relatives.

There is no doubt that the work of the billeting officers and welfare workers was impressive, though many of the dictates of the Health Minister were often overwhelmingly difficult to follow through. (For example: 'Friendly and regular visits should be made with a view to seeing that the visitors are settling down with the occupiers and that any possible causes of friction are removed at the early stage'.) Nonetheless, they worked tirelessly to do so.

If anyone was to blame for friction, in most instances it was the adults and not the children who were responsible: the parents themselves, both those who were absent and resident boarding mothers and, in many cases, intolerant foster-parents. This may seem a harsh judgement but the evidence of it is plain in the voluminous reports, both official and non-official, of the day. The child evacuees were much more flexible than their elders.

The length of time children were separated from their parents was as varied as the individuals who made the journeys. Sometimes it was for no more than two or three months (this was especially so in the Phoney War Evacuation), but in some cases separation lasted as long as two or more years. Some overseas' evacuees even remained out of the country five or six years. (When children in Britain were invited recently to contemplate the extraordinary circumstances of living away from home for such a protracted time, they were aghast. In May 1988 a Yorkshire school re-enacted Evacuation Day, 1939; a group of children dressed up as evacuees, complete with short trousers for the boys and name tags for everyone. All tended to voice the same distress: 'It would be all right to be away for one night but not for more!')*

The distances the evacuees travelled were just as varied and random as the length of time they spent away from home. From the interviews with grown-up evacuees, I learned that sometimes they travelled as little as thirty-five or forty miles (the distance from London to Berkshire, for example). A medium-length journey, perhaps from London to Bury St Edmunds in Suffolk, took many over a hundred miles from home. For others, sent from London to – say – the Cheddar Gorge in Somerset, a distance of nearly two hundred miles severed them from all that was familiar.

When the city councils assigned evacuation destinations to school parties, they did so speedily, not worrying too much about what party should go where or how. It was a very helter-skelter and, in some cases, painful procedure (two departments of a West Ham school destined for Somerset, for example, were provided with a non-corridor train – which meant no access to the toilet, of course – and the group had finally to be deposited in Wantage, Berkshire, because of the urgent calls of nature). But apart from planning

*Reported by Radio 4's 'Today' programme in a magazine item 7 May 1988.

hiccups such as this, the First Evacuation was the most impressive of all three evacuations in terms of the government's organizational skill. It proved to be the largest and the smoothest run, the realization of a blueprint-maker's dream.

In all the metropolitan areas of England and Wales, the services of 172 tube stations were used to link up with 98 mainline stations. The government paid for evacuation travelling expenses, although it was left to the county councils to tackle the thorny problem of assessing incomes and collecting the cost of billeting from the parents. Where evacuated women and children were in need (cut off from husbands and fathers serving in the forces) and unable to find the cash to finance billeting costs, aid was placed under the aegis of the Assistance Board. Provision of relief for needy or low-income families was the responsibility of the local councils.

The majority of parents, who had sent their schoolchildren away to relative safety, were working class and they found billeting costs heavy. Fathers, who were the ones expected to foot the bill from their service, factory, or other skilled or semi-skilled labouring wages, found them swingeing. If they had a part-time job mothers helped out, of course, but the responsibility of paying lay with fathers, who often discovered it was difficult to send enough money home, as well as supporting themselves in a separate place.

When fathers defaulted and mothers could not cover the expenses, grandparents could be liable for repayment. Parents were means-tested by local authorities to see if they could pay (at least twenty different tests were used nationwide), and if they couldn't, the tab was picked up by the local authority. Parents on poor relief were not expected to contribute. But as the government didn't want to appear to be 'pampering parents' who could pay, the cost of billeting children was constantly monitored and parents harried by curt official notices. Government allowances totalled £50 million a year and there was much defaulting (over £2 million arrears had accumulated by 1942). To add to the bureaucratic confusion, the task of assessing parents' capacity to pay often devolved upon school officers; that meant education suffered. The sorrow of parting from their children clearly wasn't the only pain that evacuation brought parents.

*

Naturally parents were able to visit their children to help ease the sadness of separation, but it appears the government did nothing to make visits easily available. Underlying the government's recalcitrance was a feeling that the trains and buses should be used mainly by the military: the first measure the railway companies introduced after 1 September 1939 abolished cheap day return fares! However, to quell parental complaints, especially from those mothers and fathers whose children had been sent in random fashion to faraway places such as Somerset or Dorset that were expensive to reach, one cheap ticket a month was granted each parent. (This also applied to soldiers who wished to visit their wives and babies in the evacuation areas.)

For doting parents with very young children – six and seven year olds, for instance – rationing of rail tickets must have seemed cruel. Certainly, a brisk business in rogue coach tours began to surface in 1939–40, suggesting parents did not take kindly to the restrictive government travel concessions. In a 1 July 1940 edition of the *Hackney Gazette* a news story headlined 'Trips to Evacuees' and sub-titled 'Coach Owner and Others Summoned', we read of the fining of three men from Bethnal Green and Hackney – William Baker, Sidney Crisp and Charles Winter – for organizing twice-weekly coach tours from the East End to country towns within a 60 to 100-mile radius from the capital. Northampton (Northamptonshire), Newport Pagnell (Bucks.) and Wolverton (Bucks.) are some destinations named in the report. A plainclothes policeman had nailed the shady coach operators by buying tickets and pretending to visit his evacuated family (5s for a Thursday trip, 7s on Sunday – at 20 shillings to a pound, about 25p and 35p respectively, return). Carpeted by the magistrate, Crisp, who admitted he was operating without a road service licence, said lamely that he was just 'trying to make a living'. The solicitor for the police scolded the illegal operators, noting that 'bus services to the evacuation areas . . . were strictly rationed . . . for military and other very good reasons'.

Except for Christmas and Easter, visits by parents to their children were not really smiled upon by the authorities, but tolerated as a necessary evil. There was, as the above news story reveals, a hint that one was being unpatriotic in trying to take more bus or train space than the alloted monthly visit. An exception to the monthly ration was made only in the event of an evacuee falling ill. In this case, the Ministry of Health authorized the local Assistance Boards to loan hard-up families an emergency fare.

Kathleen Thomas, my near neighbour in Leytonstone, who is a vivacious widow of sixty-five, a mother of four grown-up sons and a part-time medical secretary, told me about going to Wales to visit her younger brother and sister when they were evacuated. She was seventeen at the time, employed as a secretary in an engineering firm near her family's council flat in Stoke Newington, northeast London. Kathleen remembers:

I would have done anything for my mother. She was the salt of the earth. She hated the way our whole family had to be split up when the blitz started; she'd go around shouting 'you jack-booted gits!' every time the German planes went over, or a bomb dropped nearby. Our neighbourhood was really getting a pasting – it was the autumn of 1940 – and my Dad was very nervous. He was working on the transport lorries in the docklands and saw everything being flattened. My mother felt she should stay home with my Dad and me so my other sisters and brother were evacuated. Kitty, who was twelve, was sent to Letchworth, Herts.; June, five, and Johnny, three, went to Bargoed, Wales. Mother and I went to the station to see Johnny and June off to an 'unknown destination' as they [the authorities] put it, not telling you where for certain for security reasons. Mum put a big sign on the two of them 'Not to be separated!'. They then went to Bargoed, in Glamorgan, Wales, where they stayed with a family.

Mum was poorly so she asked me to go to Wales to see how they were. Well, of course, like everybody else in the block of flats where we lived, we were short of money. So I went along to the town hall to get a loan from what was the Lord Mayor's fund.

The official there was quite nice. The fare was just under two pounds so he made it an even two pounds. He sort of smiled and said, 'I think we can rise to the loan of the fare and give you a coffee on top.' I made sure I paid him back at the end of the month when I got my wages. My mother brought me up like that.

When June and Johnny were sent to Wales – they were there for five years – one of us usually travelled to Wales to see them at Christmas. Everything was rationed but Mum always put together a fabulous parcel – sweets, cake, storybooks, clothes, whatever she could lay her hands on. If their clothes were a bit shabby when we got there, we'd go kit them out in Bargoed. But the kids were sometimes funny when they first saw us. I remember once when Dad put out his arms to Johnny on a first meeting after a year, Johnny put his face into his foster-father's shoulder, sort of hiding. It hurt my father's feelings. The Welsh couple were very nice – called Thomas, like my married name, coincidentally enough. They were choked when they sent June and Johnny back to us in 1945.

Mum couldn't get over Johnny's strong Welsh accent when they finally came home. Johnny, especially, had got a bit stroppy. I think he missed his Welsh 'Dad'. I remember he threw some mashed potato at Mum at dinner time but she soon sorted him out. She blamed the Nazis. The war had turned Johnny into a stranger, she said. This didn't last, thank goodness.

Young Kathleen did well to organize herself a loan for her compassionate visit to Wales to see Johnny and June. The Ministry of Health would authorize a loan to visit sick evacuees only (a) upon presentation of a doctor's certificate, (b) if the family were means-tested, and (c) on receiving a promise of repayment 'in appropriate cases'. The latter clause meant that poverty-line parents need not always repay in part or in full, if real hardship was proven. In fact, no court cases took place during the war to try to recover loaned fares as it was decided that the administrative costs of doing so would be far greater than the amount of money recovered.

A foster-parent expected to receive 8s 6d (42p) each a week for looking after two unaccompanied schoolchildren up to the age of ten; 10s 6d for a single child. Taking nearly a half century's worth of inflation into account, about £10.00 a week. An Evacuation Report gives the following breakdown of billeting costs for the other age groups: ten years and under fourteen, 10s 6d a week; fourteen and under sixteen, 12s 6d a week; sixteen and over, 15s a week. The Ministry of Health memorandum regarding evacuation stated clearly that 'the primary responsibility for clothing the evacuees rests with parents'.

This single, apparently simple, rule caused much bad feeling among foster-parents through all three of the major evacuations which occurred during the five and a half years of war. Generally,

parents were lax about sending their children clothing, dottily
sending them sweets, comics and cuddly toys instead. These gifts
were received with jubilation by the children, but left their foster-
parents appalled, concerned as they were with more practical
needs such as suitable footwear to replace their charges' threadbare
plimsolls. Some foster-parents didn't take such a lofty moral stance.
One London man, sent to Brighton as an eight year old, told a
Channel 4 interviewer in *A People's War* that he had crept downstairs
from his bedroom one night, and found his surrogate parents gorging
on the sweets his mother had sent him!

It is not my purpose in this book to theorize about why, as a rule,
biological parents and foster-parents got along rather badly during
the war because I'm primarily concerned with the reactions of the
children themselves, both then and in later life, to the evacuation
experience. However, I am impressed by the comments made by
an American sociologist, Viviana A. Zelizer, regarding boarding
houses for sickly children, established in nineteenth-century New
England, to give them some protection against harsher alternatives,
such as factory shifts. Her analysis seems equally valid for the
children evacuated one hundred years later in Britain:

> Despite every effort to depict boarding as a task of love and
> regardless of the individual motivation of foster parents, the
> contractual arrangement by which families received a fee for
> the care of a child defined their task as partly commercial.
> Therefore, while boarding homes had an important part in the
> transition from instrumental to sentimental adoption, paid
> parenting remained an ambivalent occupation.

Paid parenting is never ideal and while Britain's wartime foster-
parents were hardly given exorbitant sums for their pains – one
historian has referred to the allowances as 'minimal' – it is easy to
see why the very often poor parents of evacuees from the cities
('inner-cities' in today's parlance) thought they were recompensing
country couples quite amply. They, therefore, felt irate if the in-
adequacies of their children's wardrobes were pointed out to them
time and again.

A crucial difference distinguishing those who fostered evacuated
children from the fosterers of today is that the children were not 'in
care'. They had not been abused, nor were they necessarily the
children of inadequate, wanting parents. The parents of evacuees
were doing their patriotic duty in sending their children away,

often against their will, while the foster-parents believed they were
rescuing children from danger.

There is much to suggest that those householders who took in
evacuees were indeed acting on compassionate grounds. The eight
to ten shillings a week paid for looking after a child under ten (the
largest group) might have been a small inducement for working-
class families, but it seemed barely adequate for the fussier, 'white-
lace-curtain' brigade – the lower-middle and middle-classes, whose
standards of cleanliness and dress were exactingly high for their
charges.

The bulk of the wealthier population of Britain, with some notable
exceptions (such as J. B. Priestley, who showed one young evacuee
East Ender, Justin de Villeneuve, some of the niceties of gourmet
living, see pp. 149–50) were not at all keen to accept inner-city
evacuees. Richard Titmuss has also written with some bitterness:
'As the months of evacuations dragged wearily by, a tendency for
the larger houses to be spared at the expense of the smaller ones
became more pronounced.'

A lack of co-operation from the higher-class homes was aided
and abetted by the local authorities themselves who did not lean
too heavily, if at all, upon such reluctant would-be hosts. A Ministry
of Health circular published on 8 October 1940 and sent to regional
officers grumbled that 'certain local authorities have not included
in the billeting lists the really "good class" residences'.

All of this gives credence to the antics of Evelyn Waugh's extor-
tionate anti-hero, Basil Seal, in *Put Out More Flags*, who uses the
threat of prolonged residency of a gaggle of evacuees to convince
comfortable houseowners to part with their money. In this novel,
Waugh has the Connollys – three raffish, snotty-nosed, orphaned
children called Doris, Micky and Marlene – poised as a secret
weapon aimed at the heads of hapless rural hosts. Masquerading
as a billeting officer, Seal decides to blackmail polite residents with
threats of lodging the terrible threesome in their comfortable, fire-lit
homes. Doris has 'piggy eyes' and is 'ripely pubescent'; Micky, a
little younger, is delinquent and foul-mouthed; Marlene, a year
younger than Micky, is 'simple'. Seal uses them like spanners to
wrench money from the wealthy and comfortable. Undeserving
poor – meet undeserving rich! This witty satire by an arch-
conservative was close to the reality of the day.

To be excused from taking in an evacuee all that was needed was
a medical certificate attesting to some respiratory, orthopaedic,

blood circulatory or other chronic problem, whether mild or severe. Compliant doctors abounded, leading one billeting officer to complain in 1943 that he could have plastered the façade of his university town hall with medical certificates. Feeble excuses proliferated. High-ranking government officials from the West Country and the Home Counties virtually ran for cover. One MP explained that he could not billet two secondary schoolgirls for the astonishing reason that he had too many 'confidential papers lying around'.

A report from the Association of Head Masters and Head Mistresses in July 1941, referring to evacuated grammar schoolchildren, stated acidly that 'the more well-to-do people, the superior artisan and clerk class, have tended to shirk their responsibilities'. One senior official of the Ministry of Health joined in the chorus against the shirkers in October 1941, stating that 'the real hard core is in the upper middle-classes'.

So, as the Phoney War Evacuation revealed the stark class delineations separating the inner-city evacuee children from their largely lower-middle and middle-class, foster-parents, it also spotlighted the selfishness of the upper-class living comfortably in rural areas in the southeast of Britain in particular.

Many billets were immediately satisfying to the children, especially when those of the same family were lodged together and their adjustment to their new home could be made as a group. But there was little, if any, attempt to match the 'right' child or children with 'suitable' foster-parents and some of the mismatchings were grotesque and heartless. No thought was given to the difficulties that would arise from placing Jewish children with Catholics, the very young with the old, Catholics with Protestants, atheists with the devout . . . As Susan Isaacs, the Hampstead child psychiatrist, exclaimed in her *Cambridge Evacuation Survey*: 'If only the human element had been worked out as carefully as the timetables.' (She might have been referring to the 4000 special trains used to effect the First Evacuation with clockwork precision.)

Sometimes age made no difference because the ageing couple were sensitive to the needs of their young charges, but this wasn't always the case. One billeting officer reported that a young mother and her baby were housed with a 70-year-old shepherd outside Cambridge. The shepherd was hostile to the disruption of his calm bachelor ways. And some of the foster-mothers, not having been previously assessed for their suitability as surrogate mothers, were irascible child haters. The actor Michael Caine tells of a hot-tempered, asthmatic policeman's wife with whom he was billeted in Berkshire – she delighted in punishing her unfortunate South London evacuee with severe whacks of the cane and incarceration in locked closets. He then moved on to an ageing squire who treated him gently and allowed his mother to come and clean in the 'big house'. This squire was one of the adaptable elderly foster-parents, but many others proved inflexible in the face of high-spirited children. Psychiatrists monitoring the children in the *Cambridge Evacuation Survey* agreed, perhaps unsurprisingly, that 'the over 60 foster mothers were less successful than the 40s and 50s'.

For the children, accustomed to loving grandparents, the presence of ageing foster-parents held no fears. Audrey Sparks, now fifty-three, a Kent housewife and Fleet Street executive secretary, was in no way appalled to find that her Welsh foster-parents were a vicar and his wife, both over sixty. She had loved her grandmother in her London Docklands flat and, as a result, the home she was billeted to in the Wye valley seemed pleasant in every way:

> My foster-parents didn't laugh and talk a lot the way my family did, but I didn't mind. I fell in love with their lovely house. I'd never seen anything but a Docklands council flat shaped like a rectangular box, holding a huge family of kids, myself included. I was delighted to be in a house which actually had some surprises – little curves and niches and rounded bays. Can you imagine the joy of being surprised by funny shaped walls and rooms? My foster-parents had masses of books, too, and I'd literally never seen one. I can remember the smell of snapping open a book they gave me at Christmas and inhaling its exotic aroma. And this old couple gave generous Christmas presents. I'll never forget the smell of the Christmas tree – the pine needles! What did it matter to me that they were old when they were so kind?

Audrey's evacuation experience changed her life in many ways. Before I'd discovered she'd been an eight-year-old evacuee shunted from the East End to South Wales in wartime, I'd noticed her excitement when dealing with review books sent in to the *Daily Express*'s woman's page, where I worked for three years as the Family Affairs correspondent, and she was secretary to the editor of the woman's page. She would exclaim over them, show everyone a particularly handsome cover, and flip them open and shut. I wondered at this extraordinary bibliophilia long before I interviewed her about being an evacuee. If some of the books on the joys of mechanical knitting or bottling your summer gherkins had no takers, she looked sad for a moment, but brightened when she thought of packing up the unwanteds and sending them off to the patients at St Bartholomew's Hospital nearby. Childhood deprivation had created a lifelong passion in Audrey, fostered by the ageing Welsh vicar and his wife who'd nurtured her through the war.

Like an agreeable vaccination whose effect never wears off, Audrey also loves revisiting that part of Wales where she was billeted, and returns with her husband to a luxury hotel in the Valleys almost every year. In her case a haphazard matching-up of child to foster-parents was an unqualified success. This undeniably was largely due to Audrey's youthful willingness to reach out to embrace strange ways but it also resulted from the Welsh couple's sensitivity to her; easing her into their Christmas time customs and rarely, if ever, forcing religion or bookishness upon her. If she was a child of poverty, these old people never made her feel so.

Audrey's happy experience was by no means the norm. Some of the genteel foster-parents barely disguised their disdain for the more rowdy manners of their small, street-wise guests and made their displeasure very apparent. One little girl felt these vibrations so keenly that she finally shouted: 'I'm no slum child!' Her foster-parents reported this to Susan Isaacs, presumably appalled both by the child's bluntness and at being exposed.

There was no attempt, or perhaps no time to make an attempt, to place like family with like children. A Clydeside slum child might find himself in an East Anglian country manor, waited on by maids. Little boys and girls from working-class families could be lodged with professional couples with 'plummy' accents. To add to the disharmony, few householders wanted either mothers or babies, so mothers, many of them grappling with wet, overtired infants, found themselves herded unceremoniously into college halls or draughty youth hostels.

There were language difficulties, too. In Cambridge Susan Isaacs writes:

There was a wide range of nationalities among those arriving – Austrian, French, German, Greek, Hungarian, Irish, Italian,

Yiddish-speaking Jewish, Polish, Rumanian, Russian, Siamese, Turkish (. . .) a German refugee scientist, speaking modern Greek, helped to sort out some of these problems.

Playwright Jack Rosenthal gave us one of our most enduring images of the kinds of cultural clash that occurred during the evacuations in his TV play, *The Evacuees*, screened in the 1970s. A one-time Jewish evacuee himself, he shows us how two little Ortho-dox Jewish boys evacuated from Manchester react when presented (on their first morning at the home of a crabby Protestant foster-mother) with two sizzling and obscene-looking pork sausages on their breakfast plates. This visually stunning scene was recalled innumerable times by grown-up evacuees I interviewed, even if they had no comparable sectarian jolts in their own experience, or could only vaguely remember the play.

Bernard Kops' lively Jewish mother had her own personal culture shock when she was evacuated from Bethnal Green with her children to the dales of Yorkshire, and placed in a different billet from them. Kops describes her experience in his fascinating book, *The World is a Wedding*, from his then vantage-point as a thirteen-year-old evacuee:

The next morning Phyllis and I set off to visit my mother in Nunmonkton.

I can tell you Hamsthwaite [where he and his sister were billeted] was a thriving city compared with Nunmonkton. Just lonely moorland and a dirty sky. My mother burst into tears when she saw us . . .

Phyllis tried to persuade my mother to return to Hams-thwaite with us. She didn't need much persuading, she smiled, gathered up her things, and we all set off across the fields. Me with tonsilitis and carrying two cases, or should I say strug-gling: one on my shoulder and the other knocking against my knees. Yet we weren't unhappy because we were so depressed that the only thing we could do was to laugh. And when it poured with rain we killed ourselves, my mother every so often stopping and saying with incredible incredulity, 'Nunmonkton! Nunmonkton! Nunmonkton!' She just repeated it. Her intona-tion spoke volumes. I don't wish to disparage a tiny Yorkshire village and no doubt it is the prettiest place in the world, but it is forever stencilled in my mind as the place where I reached the lowest low . . .

So we got back to Hamsthwaite. And I could have kissed every brick of those houses and even the church. Well, perhaps not. But my mother's relief at returning was short-lived, by now she was thoroughly disillusioned with the provinces.

'So what's so wonderful about fresh air?' she said. I agreed with her.

Kops and his family finally tracked down a billet in Leeds which they found more appealing: an old brothel in the infamous Chapeltown red-light district. The area was teeming with people and synagogues and delicatessens that sold bagels and dill pickles; definitely not a corner of England quite so inhabited by chilly little Protestant churches, standoffish people and acres of alien corn. 'So what's so wonderful about fresh air?'

The Kops family had their voluble mother to keep their spirits aloft, but some children had to cope with strangeness without the buffer provided by a strong maternal presence. In some cases, the mismatching almost held a Grimms fairy tale sombreness, as Derek Johnson underlines in his book, *Exodus of Children*:

There were isolated incidents where parents did forward parcels of food and clothes but unfortunately their children never did receive the contents. Such was the case of two little Essex girls who had a terrible time and nearly starved to death. Billeted with an old lady in a small country cottage they were, from the very first day, subjected to a reign of terror. 'Arriving [after a long train journey] tired, cold and very frightened all the old dear had to give us was a plate of cold mutton, mint sauce and dried bread. Very timidly we refused to eat the mutton making the excuse that we didn't eat meat anyway. We made do with the dried bread and mint sauce.

'From that day on for all the time we were there we never saw a piece of fresh meat again. On Sundays if we were very lucky we had corned beef or tinned pilchards – an absolute luxury. However, this was supposed to be a great secret and the old lady warned us that if we told anyone she would turn us into frogs! We actually believed her for after all we were only young! Even when school health inspectors called to find out how we were and why we looked so undernourished not a word passed our lips for we really did think the old dear was a witch with powers to carry out her threat!'

This addled old woman's behaviour was obviously governed by a rather terrifying caprice, not active cruelty.

Some foster-mothers profited from the relative helplessness of their young charges and exploited them as cheap labour. Mary Baxter, today a successful public relations executive of fifty-nine, who runs her own one-woman organization from a small luxury office in London's Regent Street, was eleven years old when evacuated from an outer London suburb on the Kent border to Torrington, North Devon. She remembers her evacuation experience with distaste because she was shamelessly exploited. She was sent to a rural setting of stark primitiveness, a farming hamlet miles from anywhere. Her case is yet another example of incredible mismatching as Mary, from what she describes as a 'lower-middle-class 30s semi-detached home' of some comfort and sophistication (she later went to art school and became a freelance illustrator, working for the *Standard*, as well as other papers and journals), was in no way prepared for the near 'lower depths', medieval yeomanry she discovered in her billet. (Only an outside loo and that indescribably filthy, she says). As she relates:

> I was sent off with a school party with the usual label and gas mask and so on. I found the going there very exciting but when I arrived at my billet, the culture shock was extreme. The people who inhabited this village were incomprehensible with their Devonian accents and it was like being billeted on the moon. I was placed in a workman's cottage and woke up on my first morning to the screams of a pig. I looked out of my window and saw several people beating the animal with sticks and there was a horny-handed yokel cutting the pig's throat at the same time. It was their method of killing pigs. When I asked about it later, after the shock of witnessing it, they told me that beating a pig got its circulation going so the meat would be whiter.
>
> This foster mum thought she was on to a very good thing with me and the other eleven-year-old girl billeted with her. I think she regarded it as a business transaction. We were expected to shop and wash up and look after a whining three year old.
>
> The locals thought of us as devilish, street-wise kids from London which was regarded as the centre of all evil. I used to wear cord trousers and a shirt after school and they regarded

them with horror . . . as if I was some kind of Jezebel. Being a resourceful child, I got my own back by teaching the three year old some fruity London street terms. This was one way of repaying the lady of the house for all the drudgery she was subjecting me to.

Physically, it was the most beautiful place and it probably gave me a taste for rural beauty, though I've never once returned to North Devon. I used to spend a lot of my time walking and I remember how totally desolate I felt. The primitive instincts of the locals alarmed me. Actually, it was the most disorienting period of my life, and I vowed as I walked that in the future it would be in my hands never to have such an experience again.

I went back [to London] in six months' time to the serious bombing that happened in 1941 and preferred it infinitely to North Devon.

Good experiences, bad experiences. This was the way the evacuation went. Mostly, this extraordinary event unmasked class and cultural differences as far apart as the poles. It was remarkable that a country as small as Britain should reveal such a wealth of cultural dissimilarities where, as Vera Brittain put it, describing the squalor of evacuees housed in a converted Oxford film house (see pp. 87–8): 'The applecores and the soiled newspapers will not disappear until the West End really knows and cares how the East End lives.'

As we shall see, it marked the beginning of a painful and long overdue growth in awareness. Knowledge did come, if not instant love.

3

Adult Reactions:
The Early Evacuations

Whether children were to be evacuated or not was a decision left to parents and it was a nerve-wracking one. Some historians have claimed that it might have been easier for parents if the evacuation had been made compulsory, because the 'to-send-or-not-to-send' dilemma facing them in the Phoney War Evacuation of 1939 and the Second, 'real', Evacuation of 1940 placed an enormous strain on parents. However, Churchill was opposed to making evacuation compulsory from 1940 onwards and his opposition carried the day.* The Flying Bombs Evacuation was more clear-cut: the danger in Greater London was too visible for hesitation.

The parents' reasons for keeping their children at home were easy to understand; any parent today would be able to identify with them. They feared 'the other home'; the possibility of the alienation of their children's affections by the foster-parents; the strangeness and character of the rural billet; their own difficulty in keeping in touch. Parents knew that their decision not to join the evacuation scheme was unpopular with the government, which made plain in

---

*While Churchill was opposed to making a compulsory order on evacuation, he was worried about the people's safety should they decide to stay put. As he wrote on 4 July 1940 to General Ismay: 'What is being done to encourage and assist the people living in threatened sea-ports to make suitable shelters for themselves in which they could remain during an invasion? Active measures must be taken forthwith. Officers or representatives of the local authority should go round explaining to families that if they decide not to leave in accordance with our general advice, they should remain in the cellars, and arrangements should be made to prop up the building overhead. They should be assisted in this both with advice and materials. Their gas masks should be inspected. All this must be put actively in operation from today. The process will stimulate voluntary evacuation, and at the same time make reasonable provision for those who remain.'

its poster campaigns, for example, that it thought mothers and fathers were being irresponsible if they kept their children at home.

Mass Observation (see footnote on p. 3), the team of public opinion reporters led by Tom Harrisson, canvassed the seaside towns of Southend in Essex and Felixstowe in Suffolk in May 1940 to find out why some adults refused to send their children away. MO discovered fathers were as fretful as mothers about where their children might be sent and often opted to keep their offspring with them, the risk of bombs be damned. A Southend father of a seven year old put it this way:

OBSERVER: What do people feel about evacuating children?

FATHER: People are so funny here; first they say they'll send them, then they say they won't.

OBSERVER: They don't *have* to, do they? I suppose you haven't got any?

FATHER: Yes, I've got a boy.

OBSERVER: What are you going to do?

FATHER: I'm not letting him go. They can't be looked after where they're sending them.

OBSERVER: Where's that?

FATHER: The Shires. Wales and the West.

OBSERVER: Why not?

FATHER: Well, they've nothing there; they were *starving* there *before* the war.

OBSERVER: Only the unemployed in the large towns and mining centres, surely; not in the villages.

FATHER: Well, what if I got killed? Who'd look after him? There are plenty of people here, my family and friends.

Whatever their expressed reasons – whether irrational or coolly argued – parental feelings about rejecting the evacuation scheme seemed to be characterized by guilt, confusion and belligerent self-justification. As one Felixstowe mother of thirty-five with two children of sixteen and six, told Tom Harrisson: 'We're all puzzling our heads over it,' and explained that she didn't want to have to rely on the foster-mother's letters regarding her daughter's well-being, knowing that her daughter herself would be too young to write.

The government policy of keeping destinations secret was another potent detraction to the appeal of evacuation. During the same period – the spring of 1940 – a mother of twenty-five, who lived in Felixstowe with one toddler, told the MO team: 'They send you such a long way away. You don't know where you might be landed.' This mother also made the revealing remark that Felixstowe would surely be as safe as anywhere else. (In fact, it wasn't particularly safe, but she was prescient in thinking that no port would be especially safe. Many so-called 'safe' coastal reception centres became 'unsafe' at the time of the Blitz of 1941.)

Those parents who did let their children go, both in the First and Second Evacuations, often felt nearly bereaved by the cruel, but apparently necessary, separation. Mary Collins, a *Daily Express* journalist, has described her father's reaction to her departure from London to Devon as a schoolgirl, in an article called 'The Undefeated', published on 3 September 1979, forty years after her train journey. She writes:

> My mother took me to the station. My father wouldn't come.
>
> As I left home with a gas mask hanging around my neck, a name tag pinned to my coat, and enough food to last me for five days, he lifted me up and hugged me tight, squashing my nose against his shoulder.
>
> He never spoke a word.
>
> As I walked along the street, I looked back and he was watching me from our upstairs window.
>
> I waved but he didn't wave back. He looked funny, all sad and stern, blinking a lot. I couldn't think what was the matter with him.

In many cases, when a father or mother could bear separation no longer, especially after visiting their children in a rural billet, they would recall them, offering any number of excuses to justify their action: the child 'had lost weight', 'was too homesick', 'wasn't being properly fed and washed', 'was fretting inwardly', and so on.*

Mothers, at least many of them, accompanying their pre-school children to country billets must have wondered why they'd taken the decision to be evacuated. Those questioned by MO observers at their billets in Worcester, Oxford and other provincial towns

---

*These are abbreviations of some of the reasons given for recalling children from their rural billets, printed in the *Cambridge Evacuation Survey*, 1940.

responded with a chorus of bitter complaints. They said they were being treated 'like skivvies' or, worse, as 'prisoners in their own rooms', conscious not simply of glaring class and economic differences, but of feeling extraneous.

Eva Figes, feminist and fine, evocative writer, mentions in *Little Eden: A Child at War*, an account of her life as a middle-class evacuee put up in a genteel home in Cirencester,* the impossibility of women sharing a kitchen: 'Two women do not get on well in the same kitchen, one problem that the evacuation authorities were well aware of . . .' The frequent debarring of evacuee mothers from the hosts' kitchens was often the most difficult adjustment they had to make in their new country homes. Not to be able to brew a cup of tea without supervision from a wary hostess was wearing, and sent many mothers, feeling uprooted and unattached, into the streets, cinemas and nearby cafés with their babies.

Many fastidious country wives were appalled by the sight of apparently shiftless young mothers drifting into cinemas and coffee shops, puffing on Woodbines over the tops of their babies' heads. It probably didn't occur to the rural women that the displaced mothers had few other options; they were like refugees, only they were free to leave their camps. The apathy, rootlessness and homesickness were there, without the actual lack of freedom of movement. The combination made for a sad phenomenon – the wandering mother and baby.

The plight of evacuated mothers was exacerbated by a number of circumstances. First, they missed their husbands, and secondly, their families and neighbourhoods. These dispossessed housewives from London, Liverpool and Glasgow were accustomed to a completely different way of running a household; one which was more haphazard, often more exciting and certainly noisier. When asked what they missed most, many answered – 'street markets'. The polite cluster of country market stalls in a village square or side street on a Saturday morning was a pallid affair after the joyous cacophony of Bermondsey or Walthamstow markets, for instance. Hawkers didn't vie with each other, or shout the odd *double entendre* when holding up melons, gourds or cucumbers; they didn't scream about the delights of half a pound of 'mush' (mushrooms) as they did in Whitechapel. Mothers missed the second-hand clothes blowing in the breezes on wire hangers swinging from iron rods in

*See Chapter 6, pp. 99–100.

Bethnal Green and their own neighbourhood jumble sales. These townie mothers weren't martyrs to carefully planned meals, or to needles and thread. Mending wasn't a prized pastime for them as it was in the villages, though hunting the street markets for a cheap pullover for a toddler was. Bringing up baby was a larky, communal business, accomplished in the company of friends, sisters or mothers. All the more reason why the E-Day Evacuation in 1939 seemed a desolate affair to them.

Later on in the war, when the blitzes began in earnest in the autumn of 1940, the mothers returned to the rural reception areas. They knew the danger in the cities was now real and perhaps were more amenable to the change in their lives for this reason, for they found evacuation a slightly more acceptable way of life second time around. Also, the outbreak of visible warfare appeared to alert more people to the isolation and needs of evacuee mothers, the sufferers during the Phoney War. The situation for evacuee mothers improved dramatically in 1941. Three hundred play centres were organized in the UK for the under-fives, with free lunches supplied. After this evacuee mothers could find some time in the mornings to breathe and shop and generally organize their lives; they no longer had to wander aimlessly in the towns and villages with their bored, restless toddlers.

Relationships between evacuated mothers and their country hostesses underwent a curious change, too. As the war became worse, their feelings towards each other improved. This represented a peculiar paradox but was a welcome one. But why had rural women been so hostile in the first place? As I have indicated above, sharp differences in manners and mores, cleanliness and personal hygiene, produced the strong initial antipathy.

Undoubtedly the most candid reports on what the rural housewives thought of their town guests emerged in a survey compiled in September 1940 by the National Federation of Women's Institutes and called *Town Children through Country Eyes*. The WI outlined its object in producing such a survey (the result of a questionnaire filled in by 1700 Institutes) distributed throughout those of the rural districts of England and Wales which formed most of the reception areas for evacuees:

> The material, it was felt, would be mainly useful not as regards the wartime aspect of evacuation but in solution of the long-term social problems which have been so strongly laid bare by

recent events. It was, therefore, in a constructive spirit and not with a sense of grievance that we set about the task.

Whether, indeed, it was compiled in a spirit of total objectivity is hard to tell but certainly the rural hostesses answered the question-naire in a 'gloves-off' manner, suggesting that such a forum was enormously therapeutic for them. Often, their comments tell us more about them than they do about their guests. In some, an air of moral rectitude is starkly visible, but in others saintly good nature is at work. What the Report does prove conclusively is that no one was prepared for such a dramatic social experiment.

The sleeping habits and bedwetting of the children left many of the rural hostesses gasping; also shocking to them was the lack of discipline exerted by the evacuee mothers over their children. The WI's informants conceded that damp sheets could, in part, be caused by the children's emotional reaction to uprooting, a possible awareness on their part of the teachings of Anna Freud, Sigmund Freud's daughter, who had joined the Hampstead Child Study Clinic just before the outbreak of war and had become its guiding spirit.* But their attempt to view this demonstration of apparently anti-social behaviour in an enlightened way often broke down under the onslaught of indifferent mothers, dripping sheets, soggy mattresses and the necessity of trying to dry bedding in damp country properties.

Of bedwetting, the Report states:

> The proportion varied greatly and there were reasons why it was abnormally high in September 1939. But when all the extenuating circumstances are taken into account, the fact remains that a disturbingly large number of our children must habitually be afflicted . . . Though admittedly, the predomi-nant reason was lack of home training.

The Report then proceeds to produce comments from foster-mothers to back up this finding. The towns from which the children came were also listed.

The WI countrywomen reported that the 'children relieve them-selves any time and anywhere' (this was said of both West and East

---

*Anna Freud and her colleague, Dorothy Burlingham, ran a nursery for war orphans for fifteen months and observed that bedwetting was a frequent symptom of childhood distress. They wrote about this in their book, *Children in War-Time* and their findings were widely publicized. See Chapter 9, pp. 154–6.

London children, as well as of many from the Manchester area). And mothers were not a great deal better, it seems. A description of evacuee mothers from King's Cross, London, revealed the surprising fact that the mothers were 'bedwetters', too.

Throughout the WI Report, one is continuously reminded that the children had lived chaotically in the cities, and were totally unaccustomed to routine. The girls and boys did not seem to realize that they were meant to bed down at a certain time each night. As no special time seemed scheduled for sleeping, no night clothes were worn, either. A group of evacuee children from Southampton 'put night clothes over day clothes', reported one WI worker living there. This is not to say the poor city children were unaware of domestic rituals – just that theirs were different. Richard Titmuss tells of two little Scottish town children, for example, who, when faced with white sheets on their beds in their rural billet, refused point-blank to lie on them – 'that's a bed for dead folk', they explained.

The rural gentlewomen taking care of these street-wise urchins rarely blamed the children themselves, laying the blame at the feet of their slatternly mothers instead. This might have been unfair on the mothers whose social behaviour, said the Report, 'shocked the poorest cottagers', but it probably helped the hostesses to feel compassion for the women's offspring. In their self-righteousness over the mothers' habits, however, they never considered there might be possible advantages to be found in the freer, less rigid life style of the towns, nor considered that their own might be too constricting.

The WI foster-mothers were equally astonished by the dietary habits of the evacuees. What struck them most forcibly was the fact that the children were totally unused to sitting down for meals, obviously having eaten 'on the run' all their lives. They didn't need either Colonel Sanders or the McDonalds chain to teach them that eating 'pieces' peripatetically could be fun. For a pint-size Liverpudlian or East Ender, bread and dripping eaten in the streets on the way to school was the acme of self-nourishment.

Most unnerving to many well-bred women was that the children did not appreciate 'a plain cooked meal'. They liked bread and lard for breakfast, fish and chips for lunch, and cakes for tea. What they washed their 'roe and penn'orth' down with produced more gasps – a group of child evacuees from Hull habitually drank beer! The less amusing side of their diet – if beer for the under-tens can be described as amusing – was their total ignorance of fruit and green vegetables. (Manchester evacuees were specifically mentioned in this context, but it could easily have been applicable to all, given official references to 'slum diets'.)

Incredulity mounted in the country as WI women watched their charges attempting to sup soup with knives and forks, eat eggs with their fingers, and 'whine' for bits of bread (along with chips, a favourite staple). The children frequently were not convinced that green beans, rice puddings and lamb stews were superior fare to the delicious stodge they had left behind. One eight-year-old girl evacuee in Cambridge declared: 'I miss my saveloy suppers!' (Saveloys, for the uninitiated, are thin, bright red sausages, confected in the East End, with coats of a shiny, bar-stool, red plastic hue, containing rubbery salted pork meat inside. They are an acquired taste.)

Just as the children's way of eating at table came as a revelation to their rural hosts, so did their manners and, in some cases, their morals. The overall attitude expressed in the WI Report concerning their moral standards is one of pinch-lipped tolerance – Christian, but definitely of a puritanical stamp. 'The visiting children were on the whole rougher and less disciplined than the village children . . . the art of stealing had apparently been taught the children as part of their outfit for life. The children quite expected all apple trees were public property as hedges were . . . One boy returned to his billet with a live hen under his arm and informed his landlady that he could "get plenty more" for her.'

Similar reports buzzed into the WI headquarters from around the land, indicating some disturbed sensibilities, and protesting at the children's 'bad language', 'loud behaviour' and 'lying'. Beneath all the sanctimony, however, hope and optimism for betterment illuminate the Report. These WI women were convinced they were 'civilizing' the children and improving their physical health. This hope buoyed them up and kept them going.

In the meantime, friction and clashes between town and country women continued grimly on. It inspired thousands of mothers to return home with their young. By 5 November 1939, 63 per cent of mothers and children had returned home in Scotland, and in the early winter of 1940 after the Second Evacuation, 59 per cent of all evacuated classes in Great Britain had gone back to the cities.

Cause for complaint was not the monopoly of members of the Women's Institutes. The town women didn't like their snooty, critical, house-proud hostesses any more than their rural billeters

liked them. While the country people railed against the city children
and some of their mothers as 'verminous and unclean and bedwetters to boot', rural conditions of life were often deemed sub-
standard by the city dwellers. A young middle-class mother who
wrote to MO spoke for thousands when she expressed her cause for
complaint:

> I remember so well how miserable I was then up in Scotland.
> I'd taken the children up there about a week before the war
> actually started, as I was certain it was inevitable this time,
> and like everyone else expected the most frightful blitz on
> London. We went to an ancestral mansion, which had been
> shut up for the last six years or so, and was fifteen miles from
> the nearest town.
> I had no car, and the few tiny shops in the nearby village
> were impossible. None of the windows in the house would open
> properly. Everything was soaking damp all the time. There
> was no electricity or gas. Newspapers didn't arrive until after
> tea, and it took me five days to hire a wireless which even then
> didn't work properly. There was no room, no enclosed space
> out of doors where it was safe to leave the children and,
> of course, there were no cots, playpens, and all the other
> paraphernalia of children.
> What was worse, I had only been able to bring two of
> everything in the way of children's garments and nappies so
> that I seemed to spend the entire time washing and ironing.
> Owing to the general upset, it was impossible to get any
> furniture and luggage sent from home for a month. I nearly
> went mad with complete solitude all the time and the awful
> difficulties of managing the children without any facilities
> whatever. In the end, the older one got ill, I think probably
> from bad milk as, judging by the smell of the local dairy, they
> had not washed out the bottles for years and as the perpetual
> chill and dampness was the worst thing possible for her, we
> left.

In their zeal to accumulate good letters, the MO observers didn't
always publish such important journalistic details as how many
children their correspondents had or their ages. However, it is clear
this young mother had several and that she found her surroundings
primitive and trying. To consider the late arrival of daily newspapers

a grave wartime hardship is absurd, but everything is relative, and
obviously the Blitz did seem bearable by comparison.

But while this sophisticated mother bemoaned her own lack of
comfort in Scotland in a rather self-centred way, a Cricklewood
housewife, writing to the MO team from the Midlands, enumerated
some of the very real problems of evacuation in a more objective
tone. She wrote in November 1939:

> Washing day seems more important to people in the country.
> Children were sent to school obviously ill because they would
> be a nuisance around the place on such an important occasion.
> Most of our children seem very content with their billets, but
> they miss their parents a great deal, but I have heard many
> reverse stories.
>
> The teacher's plight was even worse than the children's.
> While I was away [from the village] there was no intellectual
> or social advantage offered by anyone. The blackout makes
> visiting in the country very difficult nowadays. The main
> drawback was that one's room in someone else's house was not
> one's own place. No one dared to ask another person inside
> the front door. The attitude all round, this governs perhaps
> sixty teachers and helpers, was 'I *have* to put up with you –
> and that's as far as I'm going.' It's very rare that evacuees
> are genuinely welcomed. On the other hand, many hostesses
> started with the intention to do their utmost to make their
> erstwhile guests happy. Most of them tried too hard and got
> tired.

Gossip erupted two months or so after the First Evacuation with
village stories about town mothers reaching grotesquely hostile
proportions; a corresponding lack of sympathy for country ways
became evident among city mothers. A Gerrards Cross, Bucks.
hostess and voluntary helper had this to say to the MO reporter
about the evacuees in the autumn of 1939:

> I have been helping with the children and with some of the
> mothers, so I have had the opportunity of observing their
> attitude. They have the slum mentality, all right. Do as little
> as you can and take as much. One woman actually dared to
> say to a member of the household who took her in 'you are
> paid to wait on me'.

Another report from Bungay gave full vent to widely circulating prejudices:

There are reports of women fighting in the streets. I gather they only fight each other, not the women they are billeted on. Apparently the women at Reedon use bad language all day, but at night they put their children away and go out and get drunk, and then their language is even worse and they terrorise the village, wandering about the streets shouting and singing and swearing and keeping everyone awake. Mrs A. at Abderby (Suffolk) said that it was the country that got most of them down, as one of them said to her 'the country is one of the things you've got to put up with when there's a war'.

Even tolerant attitudes to child evacuees broke down on occasion, as an Essex MO diary extract makes plain:

One of the Town Hall staff had a story to tell about his evacuees. He was married about fifteen months ago, and of course had new furniture. Now his dining room chairs have seats in tatters, the child evacuee stands on them, and picks at the fabric to make big holes. The kid even ties a skipping rope between two chairs and skips to her heart's content. I need not say what happens when she trips over the rope. The newly distempered walls are covered with dirt and the house is in a terrible state.

One of the most absorbing aspects of the evacuation is that it seemed to inspire such conflicting attitudes. The old adage, 'One man's meat is another man's poison', was never more true than with evacuated mothers. Mrs Ivy Moore is a lively mother of two and a grandmother, aged seventy-six, living at Whipps Cross, East London. She told me of her London exodus and country billet with dancing eyes:

I was living in Lambeth in the late 30s and became part of the September 1st scheduled evacuation. My son and I were billeted at a lovely village pub called 'The King's Arms' in the village of Langton Matravers in Dorset. It was so entirely different to see rolling green hills, cows and sheep, instead of the grim bricks and mortar that was Lambeth. My son was five years old and I was twenty-six. They were very kind and loving towards us. My son adjusted to it – he went to a good school there – and I straight away thought it was like paradise, especially after what we had left behind. My son and I were never homesick and never wanted to go back to London. We were too happy enjoying the beautiful scenery. It has given us an enduring love of Dorset. To cap everything, I had a wonderful job as a laboratory assistant at the Technical Research Establishment there.

We were away almost six years but we had to come back to London as my home was there and all my belongings. We returned the year war ended under duress from my family. I was not shocked by the bomb damage as I had lived among it from time to time when visiting my parents. But I never did feel cut off from my family as Dorset was the love of my son's life and mine. I look back at my time there as one full of happiness and love – in fact, as far as I'm concerned, Langton Matravers is 'Paradise Lost'.

Ivy Moore's enchantment with her evacuation experience was not the norm with mothers, as we have seen, though it is pleasant to know that some came away with an arcadian vision of the countryside. Many children certainly took to it readily, but enraptured mothers were rarer. Some observers believed they were being stubborn and unimaginative in not making a better adjustment.

The mothers in rural billets often 'lacked any central guidance or strong stimulation from above', Tom Harrisson, the MO team leader, opined in an article printed in an industrial magazine in December 1939. He was barely able to mask his disapproval of what he described as their empty 'leisure culture'. There is no doubt that they did flee to the pubs and cinemas whenever they could, flocking to the escapist movies that proliferated at the time: stories of burning cities and flaming lust in Atlanta (*Gone with the Wind*); frustrated passions on the moors (*Wuthering Heights*); and cosy warblings on Main Street, USA (*Three Smart Girls Grow Up*). In Tom Harrisson's words:

> City women largely hate evacuation. Over half of them have either prevented their children being evacuated or have brought them back.
>
> Recent work in Liverpool has shown that of those whose children are still away – 38% of women with some children away are definitely made unhappy thereby; 54% of women with all their children away are definitely made unhappy thereby; only 11% are glad their children are evacuated,

although 94% specifically say their evacuated children are very happy.

Evacuation had introduced a new insecurity into women's lives and into this war a new horror angle, fear of bombs, often felt only most privately and not healed by holding on to your child. That feeling severely interfered with the evacuation scheme.

Disillusionment with the evacuation; a fear of bombs which threatened to fall and yet did not materialize – unmistakably, a great many mothers were feeling dispirited, bewildered and a little tired of being exhorted to remain cheerful and brave when bad news beat in upon them, relentlessly, from their wirelesses. The collapse of the French forces during the spring of 1940 which led, inexorably, to that country's official capitulation on 22 June seemed a slow-motion nightmare to women in British cities.

In the late spring of 1940, a housewife jotted down these reflections in a diary later put on file by the MO team:

It will need a miracle of strategy to get us out of the jam in which we now find ourselves. Any day now we may be mercilessly bombed as they are bombing open towns in France and Belgium. Their aim is the Channel ports and then the great onslaught on this country. American reports say that when Hitler gets the Channel ports he will call on this country to surrender. What a hope, little Adolfer, we would sooner die.

My own feeling is one of amazement that we, the British, should find ourselves in a deadliner like this. How has it come about? We thought France was almost impregnable with her famous Maginot Line, which does not seem to be playing any part at all in the present struggle. It makes one realise that we have not used the eight months' respite to the best advantage. Someone has bungled and badly, but here again I must withhold criticism. The country seems to have awakened at last to the danger on our very doorstep. Let us hope it is not too late. We are facing the biggest crisis in our civilisation, may God help us, we need help as never before.

The women's magazines of the day were impatient with such defeatist-sounding thoughts. They 'tom-tomed' out cheery encouragement, and tips for keeping one's spirits aloft ('Keep your ankles warm'; 'Carry barley sugar around should you get tired travelling';

'Have a thrifty Christmas'; 'Do not neglect the products of the hedgerow' (for cooking); 'Welcome the children' (evacuees); 'Grow fit not fat on [your] war diet!' (from a 1940 Ministry of Food entreaty published by *Woman's Journal*).*

But in spite of the growing menace across the Channel, the wisdom of the evacuation was questioned by some who were not entirely happy with the spectacle of lonely, unmotivated women trying to adjust to the stringencies of rural billeting. A Suffolk housewife, aged fifty, was pleased at the progress of 'her' evacuee, who had grown 'fat and well and assured' she reported to MO, but she added this grave reservation:

> On the whole, the local people are very kind to the evacuees, but do find many of them terribly restless and easily 'bored' and not well-disciplined. However, most have remained, and they all look better. Most people here feel it is a *faute-de-mieux* policy, and that it would be better to take large empty houses no longer used by the 'military', and let the mothers of these families come too.

No amount of official encouragement and media pleas for 'smiling through' could possibly eradicate such sensible doubts and reasoned heart-searchings. Fifty years later, history tends to offer up a blanket picture of cheery 'blitz spirits' at the grassroots' level. But the MO's populist findings indicate there never was a lemming-like 'we'll-all-go-down-together-when-we-go' acceptance of the war at work in people's minds, in spite of the incredible valour some displayed.

The children, too, did not accept the war in any uniform, all pervasive way.

*From *Women in Wartime*, see Sources, p.170.

4

The Children's Thoughts about Evacuation and War

Rural hosts were so stunned by their small, raggedy and unruly charges, they probably did not realize that the children regarded *them* with consternation, too. What was considered a safe retreat from bombs by a government planner could look like a landscape on the other side of the moon to a city child.

Fortunately for posterity, the children's reactions to the E-Day Evacuation and those that followed, as well as to the war itself, were well documented by roving MO journalists, and also by teams of teachers and child psychologists.*

One reaction shared by the evacuees which is pronounced in these early reports, indicates that the children maintained a strong sense of identification with their kin back home, and no startling change in status, taking them from a city slum to a country manor, could shake loose such a fundamental attachment. Evacuees rarely seemed to lose sight of the fact that their foster-parents were just that, foster-parents. In those cases where a child did shift his or her affections from the natural parents to the adoptive ones, this resulted from a lengthy period of separation at too young an age, and/or evacuation without the mother. This happened, as I have mentioned, to Kathleen Thomas's toddler brother, Johnny, who was away from his parents in Wales for nearly five years (see Chapter

*Researching the material, I was astounded at the amount of commentary gathered in 1939–40, which definitely tapers off during the course of the war, regarding subsequent evacuations. I can only assume that scholars and reporters grew accustomed to the phenomenon as the war went on. A parallel can be made, I think, with the shocked and obsessive media attention devoted to the impact of the war on the minds of children in Northern Ireland during the 70s; such interest is much rarer now in the 80s.

2, pp. 24–5). It is significant that only a small number of adoptions took place during the evacuations. (As Dr Carlton Jackson points out this was not, however, always the case with evacuees sent overseas to North America, Australia, South Africa or New Zealand, especially if the evacuation period extended over four years. The sheer geographical distance involved, and the total uprooting to another land, did often make the children feel emotionally distant from their biological parents.)

What particularly struck me during many of my interviews with the grown-up graduates of the evacuation experience was how impervious they had been to the spoiling and blandishments of wealthy foster-parents. Even at a very young age, they could mourn for a 'Nan' back home in South London, and while maintaining excellent manners with their hosts, never lose sight of who they were and to whom they belonged. As a group the evacuees were a proud, independent bunch.

Kathy Tuffin, a 53-year-old civil servant and grandmother living in Catford, South London, vividly remembers her evacuation since she was whisked to Wollfold, Lancashire at the tender age of eight. She had been living with her kindly grandparents in Bromley, Kent when the bombs started dropping with deadly regularity on London.

My grandparents were poor people. I remember them saying, 'Please God, spare us,' when the bombs dropped in autumn 1940, I'm sure it was. I was evacuated with a neighbourhood friend and my brother and I remember the train trip as being a bit of a nightmare because we were so thirsty. When we got to Lancashire, we were herded into Wollfold Community Hall and saw these ladies preparing sandwiches and cakes for tea. But we cried out for water – we didn't want food. We were like cattle being auctioned. My brother says he must have been an ugly mutt because he was the last to go and as I wouldn't leave without him, I was among the last, too. I must have looked a sight. All I had in the world was a brown paper parcel and a brown paper carrier bag. I had one pair of knickers and that was it. I had no toothbrush. My grandmother had made me a flannel out of flannelette sheeting.

I can't remember if the couple who picked me showed their shock at my appearance. They must have hidden it if they were shocked. They took me to their lovely home and I was given my own bedroom. They also gave me a Scotch terrier and I'd never had a pet before. We went to Sunday school and church on Sundays and I was given tripe and onions for the first time. I thought it was delicious and I probably gained weight over the months. But I missed my grandmother and mother terribly.

The village was like another world – all cotton mills where I went. The women wore clogs and shawls over their shoulders – you could hear the clogs shuffling down the road in the mornings. School was peculiar, too. The classrooms had big, old-fashioned, framed desks and the floor sloped higher in the back. I was told to sit in the front of this sloping room. I couldn't understand the Lancashire accent and this terrified me so I started to cry. A few days later they switched me to a class with younger children. They had trouble sorting us out.

My foster-parents were very kind. They gave me the first holiday I'd ever had. We went to Blackpool. But I only stayed about nine months with them. I missed my family too much. Also, I felt self-conscious and frightened of the unknown. I've often worried about whether the couple liked me or not.

It is certain that sometimes foster-parents, especially when they were childless, like those who cared for Kathy Tuffin, must have felt rebuffed when their small charges went home with such alacrity, without a backward look. Nine months in an eight year old's life is a long time, but nothing dimmed Kathy's longing to get back to Bromley, bomb-ravaged as it was.

Some of the older evacuees made no secret of their objection to being sent away. Of the many evacuees I interviewed, the one who stayed away the shortest time was an Edinburgh friend of mine, Shelagh Metcalf, wife of a retired advertising executive living in Wisborough Green, Sussex, and mother of two. Sent in 1940 to a small hamlet far north of Edinburgh with a cousin when she was eleven, she decided to go home to her mother after twenty-four hours: 'I simply staggered to the nearest kiosk,' she told me, 'and rang her, saying it was all impossible. She didn't protest at all so I went straight home.'

Evacuees had very black-and-white views as to why their billets attracted or offended them. Susan Isaacs, in her *Cambridge Evacuation Survey*, took careful note of the opinions of the 300 or so evacuee schoolchildren from Islington and Tottenham, who resided in

Cambridge in the Second Evacuation of 1940. She enlisted the help of
two teams of teachers to find out how they were adjusting, by asking
the children to write two essays, one on 'What I Like in Cambridge'
and the other on 'What I Miss in Cambridge'. The replies from the
group – aged eight to fourteen – about what they liked and what
they missed were refreshingly candid. One fourteen-year-old girl
stated her criticism with blazing simplicity: 'Cambridge people, in
most cases, are snobs.'

The things they commented on would have startled their London
parents. A fourteen-year-old boy confessed: 'I like my brothers and
sisters being at home and not messing up my belongings . . . I miss
getting hidings from my dad when I get into trouble.' This boy's
preferences also indicated an incorruptible love of the city, 'I miss
the thunder of the tube in the underground.'

A finicky loathing of Cambridge cyclists and bad driving per-
meated quite a few of the young respondents' essays. Said one
nine-year-old boy: 'I dislike the people who show off on bikes and
skates.' And another ten-year-old boy wrote, 'The things I do not
like in Cambridge is that the traffic is crowded in the road and
people are easily knocked over.' And, then, there was this rather
damning assessment from a lofty-minded fourteen-year-old boy:
'The bus service in Cambridge is greatly inferior to the London
Transport Service. The streets, in places, are very narrow and
crowded with traffic and pedestrians which makes it very dangerous.
Also the danger is increased by the fact that the drivers of buses,
being used to it, take unnecessary risks.' Another road-safety-
conscious boy of thirteen added: 'There are *no* tramlines here, to
the danger of cyclists on wet days.'

These North London children were frequently placed in rather
grand manor houses employing maids, and this led to some mixed
reactions. One fourteen-year-old girl was not impressed: 'I am
sometimes unhappy at my billet, as the maids quarrel a lot and
make it awkward for us.' A twelve-year-old girl offered a contrasting
view: 'I have all our meals with the maids and not with the lady of
the house. The maids are very nice.'

The posh food served in the big houses also received some mixed
reviews. Wrote one fourteen-year-old girl, 'We have very nice food
such as venison, pheasant, hare and other luxuries which we cannot
afford at home,' but a girl classmate of hers of the same age was
not quite sure about such fare, 'I also miss my proper English food
because my people are continental, and so their taste is much

different to ours.' In the same vein, another fourteen-year-old girl thought, 'The dinners where we are staying are much more richer than we have at home.'

What the children missed about home and family was often curious. Teasing and messy play, the signs of a freer, rowdier background, were high on the list, as one seven-year-old girl made clear: 'I miss dolls Pram and mummy and daddy and granma and bathing her [the doll] at night and putting her to bed and put cums down her throat and bits of fish and dressing her in the morning and put her plats in and cloming her hair and nursing her.' One thirteen-year-old regretfully remembered her brother: 'I miss my brother always teasing me.' And another thirteen-year-old shared her feelings: 'Although it feels nice not to be teased, I'm afraid I miss it.'

Young teenage boys often said they missed their garden shed back in the city. This, among other things, featured in the complaints of a thirteen-year-old: 'I miss Dad's shed . . . We have no tools in my billet here. I miss the electric light in my bedroom, we use candles here. I miss my sink at home, we have to go outside and wash under a tap here.'

Other more esoteric pleasures apparently absent in Cambridge caused some young teenagers to pine. A fourteen-year-old boy said he missed his father's Sunday Communist Party meetings, and another his own science experiments, which he was unable to pursue in his billet because his room was too small.

That acres of countryside could not compensate in some children's minds for neat patches of urban parkland was also evident. One seven-year-old girl stated firmly, 'I miss the parks' (she wrote this and nothing more). The same note of nostalgia crept into a thirteen-year-old boy's complaint: 'I miss my patch of garden.' Echoing their sentiments, a fifteen year old summed it up: 'I miss all the recreation ground.'

But the children were not by any means utterly negative about their new homes. One eight-year-old boy became quite lyrical about what he liked about Cambridge, noting: 'Cauliflower. Sweets. Country walks. Pets. Apples.' Apples gained their wholesale approval with a thirteen year old raving, 'I like the meals which I am having in my billet, the best of all apple dishes made with apples.'

They also liked the undergraduates, finding them informal and zany. Judging from their comments, the Cambridge curates and vicars made a resounding hit, too. The words of a seven-year-old

boy: 'I also like the choir . . . I like the vicar. I like him because he
is kind to me,' would have found favour with a thirteen-year-old
girl who wrote, 'I like the vicar and the curate at the church which
I attend better than the one at home.'

Kindly vicars, choirs, apples, venison, country walks. In spite of
the children's reservations, the Cambridge evacuation sounds an
orderly, pleasant and reasonably successful affair. In large measure,
this resulted from unaccompanied children travelling there in school
groups with familiar school-teachers in charge. Consequently, a
sense of cohesiveness and continuity was maintained in their lives;
they were never allowed to feel abandoned or isolated, as little
Kathy Tuffin did in Lancashire, for example, where she felt over-
whelmed by the strangeness of her new school and the northern
accents.*

Homesickness was an acute problem with many evacuees. One
grown-up evacuee recalled that she always smuggled a small hair-
bow her mother had given her into her pyjama pocket at night. In
order to sleep, she would put it on her pillow and rub it against her
cheek for comfort. It had been a gift, casually given to her by
her mother to dress-up with, but it gained enormous emotional
importance as the months in her new billet stretched from the
autumn of 1939 into the summer of 1940, whereupon her mother
fetched her back to London (foolishly, as it turned out, since the
bombs began to drop savagely then). She felt guilty for not being
able to warm to her foster-mother, but she also recalls feeling
actively repelled, at eight, by this well-meaning woman's goodnight
kiss. The little girl thought she smelled of disinfectant – at any rate,
nothing like her real mother.

Even the most well-behaved children could feel baffled and angry
by their half-understood separation from a beloved home. They had
been asked to be brave, to shuffle off into the unknown, but that
couldn't prevent a great deal of bewilderment and anger from
engulfing them. If the grown-ups hardly knew why they had been
forced to separate themselves from their children, how much less
could their children be expected to understand what had happened
to them! Often, evacuation did not seem a 'larky' adventure, but a
minor tragedy, ill-comprehended and deeply resented.

Dr Isaacs was profoundly sensitive to their emotions. She quite
correctly believed that young adolescents could adjust better if

*See pp. 50–51.

they knew that evacuation wasn't pleasant for anyone, neither for themselves nor their parents. She cited the case of Rose, aged thirteen, who returned home to Tottenham, North London, on 23 November 1939, after only eleven weeks at her billet. Her father was a poor tailor and often out of work; her mother made boxes at piece-work rates of pay. The home was humble but immaculate, the Isaacs team reported, and the family's payments to the foster-home had been sent through the Unemployment Assistance Board. Susan Isaacs described the complex feelings the mother and daughter had experienced when Rose had been evacuated:

> Rose is the eldest child in a family of three girls. Her mother, described as 'a very pleasant and quiet woman', said that Rose 'fretted inwardly' whilst she was away. It had been reported to the mother by friends visiting Cambridge that she was looking ill because of homesickness, so she decided to bring her home. Subsequently, she heard from a younger girl that Rose cried herself to sleep every night 'for fear of what could happen to them if father and mother were killed in London'. The mother herself had visited Rose twice in eleven weeks, and she had no complaint to make about her billet, though she is inclined to think that it is best for children to stay with their parents, and would not consider sending this child away again . . .

Sometimes, mothers attributed emotional distress to their children that had less to do with the child's lack of adjustment to evacuation, than its mother's feelings of bruised *amour-propre* in her dealings with her offspring's new foster-parents. London mothers were frequently on the alert for what they feared might be slights and snooty treatment and were quick to answer in kind. Dick's mother adopted this tactic. He was returned to his home in Islington after a mere eight weeks' stay with his Cambridge foster-parents. Dick's father was a moderately successful builder of costers' barrows, and his parents visited him three times after he was evacuated on 3 September 1939. The Isaacs team had this to say about his stay there:

> Dick was the second child in a family of four, of whom the elder brother, aged fourteen, billeted separately, was not brought home and a sister, aged eight, had been taken home earlier. A five-year-old brother was not sent away at all.

Dick [aged nine] had had one change of billet, due to overcrowding. He had been placed with four other children, and the hostess said she could not cope with so many for reasons of health.

The mother complained that in the billet the child was not kept clean: his ears were dirty, and his clothing was not properly washed. Every time the parents visited he was unhappy and cried to come home. (The school record confirmed the fact that the child had been homesick.) The mother said that he was obviously not wanted and both parents felt that this was bad for him. The billet, they said, consisted of an elderly couple over seventy, and one unmarried daughter. They had been accustomed to undergraduate lodgers and resented the reduction of income and the increased responsibility of having children.

Summarizing her own impressions, the investigator added: 'Above reasons are in order given by mother with strong feeling. The last point was developed in the interview, and appeared the really important one. Parents resented the attitude of concession on the part of the hostess, and "being made to feel like paupers".'

Dick's story is significant because it seems to contain all the ingredients that made for the worst billets: an over-age foster-couple at the helm; financial considerations too much in evidence on the part of the hosts; an over-dependent child in the billet with over-anxious, clinging parents at home, eager to spot slights. Apparently, one of the great grievances nurtured in this family centred round allegations made by the foster-parents that 'some compensation' should be paid to them for 'wear and tear' on their furniture. The London mother was incensed, saying that the furniture sagged and appeared to have been with the couple 'all their married lives'!

Often, it was the teachers, not the parents, who ensured the smooth transition of children from home to billet. They would fight long and hard to see that some equilibrium and comfort were maintained in the children's lives in spite of the chaos that so often threatened to overwhelm them.

In his wartime diary, Eric Wyeth Gadd, a Southampton schoolmaster, described the trials he encountered trying to set up a proper, part-time school for evacuees there. Gadd was first put in charge of an influx of evacuees in 1939; later, he coped with a second onslaught of children in June 1940. Southampton was one of the many port towns in Britain which at the outset of the war was designated a 'safe area', but which turned into a danger zone as its strategic maritime importance became evident to the Germans. However, while this Hampshire town retained its standing as a 'safe' destination for evacuees, Gadd worked tirelessly to improve schooling conditions. His diary entry dated 30 June 1940, records his dedication:

> During the past month I have been conducting a private war with the County Education Officer on a matter which I regard as of vital importance: the grave risks which are being run by the children attending the Gore Road Junior School there.
> I have put forward these points:
> 1. The building is an ex-army hut – a relic of the last war. Having been in use continuously for about twenty years, it is in a dilapidated condition.
> 2. It is constructed entirely of wood, with the exception of the roof; the walls are of thin matchboarding and weatherboard of a combined thickness of about one inch and in no way reinforced.
> 3. The lighting system is of gas.
> 4. The roof is low, solid and heavy.
> 5. The building is less than 400 yards from the main Southern railway line.
> Leaving aside the effect of a direct hit, this building would be vulnerable even to the effect of a bomb dropped anywhere within half a mile, while an incendiary could have unthinkable results.

In spite of the powerful case he presented to the Southampton Education Secretary, involving much correspondence and a great deal of righteous hectoring on his part, he was only able to convince the authorities to build air-raid shelters in a corner of the playground. The history of the evacuations is filled with such Kafka-esque stories – lone, unsung heroes battling with the forces of bureaucracy; intractable officials, who were often inflexible or apparently unco-operative because they had little idea where their real duties lay and no spare funds to carry them out, even had they wished to do so.

The hit-or-miss attitude to schooling, plus the lack of adequate accommodation, appealed, however, to many young evacuees. Boys and girls, who had been used to fairly strict timetables and all-day lessons in London or Birmingham, suddenly found themselves with free mornings and only two or three hours of study in the afternoon. (Evacuees had to fit into the routine of the village schools as best they could; understaffing and lack of facilities frequently meant curtailed teaching or afternoon lessons only.)

Harry Salmon was seven years old when war broke out. His home was in East Ham, East London: his evacuation to Warminster, Wilts. brought with it an end to regular schooling and the beginning of a marvellous break. Harry, now fifty-three, a grandfather and the manager of an off-licence in Leyton, East London, looks back at his evacuation year with a mixture of pleasure and some trepidation. He says it left 'some scars', but he won't define them. A valued member of the Leyton community – he was a leader of the borough's fight against a 62 per cent council rate rise in 1987 – if he does have some scars, they don't show. He describes his experience of 1 September 1939 and the ensuing year, as follows:

I went to Warminster, Wiltshire with a school. I stood all the way on the train with a big bar of Cadbury chocolate in my pocket, a gas mask and a cardboard box. We walked from our school in the southern part of East Ham to Upton Park. Kids were giving us sweets as we walked by – fruit and stuff. My mother came with me as far as the local underground station. We took the tube to Paddington station from there. I felt a bit weepy at first, but I was too excited to worry very much about it. When we got to Warminster, we all piled into a church hall. I was almost immediately picked out by a family.

I was assigned to a lovely place – a big house with a swimming pool and orchards. It was a lot different to what I'd known – I'd come from a two-up, two-down house with no bathroom. My host was a major in the artillery and his house was out of this world, I thought. They had a maid, and a daughter called Pauline, who was my age and we got on very well. As far as the food went, there wasn't anything that I hadn't seen before, but there was just a lot more of it and it was served differently. I wasn't used to such an abundance of food.

My mother came to visit me, then I wanted to go home. The main thing I remember was that we didn't go to school very much and that pleased me terrifically. We'd go to the school, all right, but then the teacher would take us for walks. We never seemed to have any formal lessons. We used to cross a field to go to the school and we'd rush away to avoid a cow. I thought that was a rare sight.

I was in this mansion with all the luxuries and opposite me was a girl who used to live in East Ham. She had a modern house in the East End and here she was in a tiny little cottage. We'd reversed our life styles.

I've always had a yearning to go back and see the house again and the countryside, but I've never done it. I'm a terrible city boy, I suppose. It's the silence that gets me about the country – I can't stand it. Back in the 6os, I was convalescing in a Harlow hospital from a routine operation – Harlow was more countrified then – and the silence afflicted me again – no cars, no sirens, terrible! Stupid, isn't it?

But though I hated the silence, you couldn't say the experience was unsettling with any bad effects or anything. The big shock was going home a year later after the Battle of Britain. There wasn't a window in the house. All of them were out and done up in black tarpaulin. I thought to myself, 'What have I come back to?'

Haphazard as their education was, it did not appear to have any lasting ill effects on the evacuees, except in some cases on their grammar and spelling. The atmosphere (and silence!) of the countryside seems to have engraved itself on their memories more than their truncated lessons.

Once back home in London and the other big cities, children had more time to reflect on the effects of war itself, rather than on what their rural billets had had to offer, or what they'd lacked. One of the chief contributions the MO reporters made during the war was to ask children what they thought about what was happening around them. Blunt questions about the blackouts, evacuation, the Germans, Hitler, the threat of blitzkrieg in 1939 and its reality in 1940 were all put to London schoolchildren, aged nine to fourteen. The MO canvassers believed that children frequently mirrored the opinions of their parents and, while this is undoubtedly true with some deep-seated prejudices (hatred of Hitler, for example), many of the replies contain the quirky, off-beat flavour of a child's own perception of events. Happily, the MO observers let the children ramble on at will, eagerly jotting down what they were told – misconceptions, fantasies, exaggerations . . . As most of the questioning took place on the streets in the East End, one assumes answers came from less well-off children: from those who either never had been evacuated, or else from those who had been, but had since returned home.

The children appear to have been aware of Hitler's victories in the first year of the war: they would, after all, have seen him repeatedly in newsreels, since Pathé and Paramount news footage was regularly screened for ten to twenty minutes alongside feature films in the movie houses. During the war, Saturday afternoon at the local cinema was a highlight of most children's weekends in the East End, with early Walt Disney films providing a constant diet of fun and laughter – *Fantasia* was released early in 1940, and *The Three Little Pigs*, although released in the late 30s, was a perennial favourite throughout the war. Therefore, a kaleidoscopic jumble of clips showing the ubiquitous Hitler, along with films starring Pluto, Mickey Mouse, Donald Duck and the Sugar Plum fairy, would have been familiar to almost every city child.

Hitler also became part of city children's dreams, or nightmares; he lodged in their psyches the way a pop superstar does today. His silly, toothbrush moustache and neat, oily head were as much a part of their internal imagery as Michael Jackson's pretty melancholia and black stetson hat are for young people in the 1980s. Hitler never kept a low profile, but was a very visible, omnipresent bogey-man. While everyone would have seen him in films, haranguing the Party faithful from a podium in pre-war Nuremberg, Berlin or Munich, the children would also have seen many sequences showing his army's seemingly inexorable march to total victory.

Newsreels would have shown them the train coach at Compiègne where, on 22 June 1940, Hitler forced the French to sign papers setting out their own surrender. As the authors of the book *All Our Yesterdays* have pointed out: '. . . Hitler, with the instinct of the showman, dictated them [the surrender papers] in the railway carriage at Compiègne where the defeated Germans had had to surrender to Marshal Foch in November 1918'. Here was a devil children could understand, if not identify with. He rubbed his enemies' noses in their own failures, and then danced a little jig! No sinister cartoon character out of *Dandy*, *Beano* or a Walt Disney film could have done it better. To a British child's mind, it must have seemed as if an evil genie was dancing demonically on the grave of everyone's hopes. For the children of his day, Hitler existed in a land where fantasy and reality overlapped and finally merged.

One of the leading questions MO put to random children was: 'What do you think about the war?' Boys' feelings veered from the openly fearful about the outcome of the war to the frankly sadistic where Hitler was concerned. Eric, ten, took quite a cool, adult view, strongly tinged with Christian overtones, but apprehensive nonetheless:

> War is terrible because men get killed. Hitler is wicked. He wants everything in the world that doesn't belong to him; he takes things in the devil's way and not God's way. But we'll come out all right in the end, and we want to put all our men in Germany, so that the Germans can't make another war, and we can live in peace.

Sometimes the boys' replies were brisk, cryptic, and to the point. John, aged ten, thought: 'Hitler's a rat, because he kills so many people – they haven't done him any harm'; while an essay, written for MO by a fourteen-year-old Stepney boy, so pulsated with violent images that the reporter apologized in his commentary upon it for its 'sadistic thoughts'. The boy wrote with relish:

> If Hitler was captured, the best death for him would be dreadful torture. The best way to make him die would be to put him in plaster of Paris, and make him suffer such agony that he would be glad to be got out of it. His hair would be set alight that it would be all burned off. His moustache would be singed off his face . . . Every day a bit would be taken off him, of what remains then when he is half-dying he would be torn with pincers and executed. The same would happen to Mussolini, Mosley, Goering, Goebbels, Ciano, Ribbentrop, Claudius and Ley, also Himmler.

It is curious to see that this hopelessly bad speller, if vivid thinker, managed to mix up history's villains: somehow a Roman emperor (Claudius) was also destined to die a horrible death for his outrages against humanity. Passionate, confused thinking of this sort abounded.

In 1939 and 1940 during the Phoney War, some children – boys, in particular – felt restless. Where was the action, they wanted to know. One eight year old couldn't suppress his disappointment on 25 April 1940, even though he was probably aware that the Norwegians were losing, 'It doesn't seem to be a war, does it? Where is the war? Are they fighting it out at sea?' Some of the boys also expressed disappointment at the lack of air raids and bombs. It was all smoke and little fire. Even Hitler, the Evil One himself, was called upon to stir things up. Said one ten year old, engagingly, 'Hitler, would you be a dear and bomb my school, please? Then I'd give him six shillings for bombing it.'

Hitler's evil reputation, and his apparent hold over Europe, affected the girls somewhat differently. They didn't devise tortures for him; the tendency was more for the despot to enter *their* dreams. The practical necessities of war unsettled them – blackouts, rationing and evacuation – and while Hitler was a definite bugbear in their minds, too, their comments were free from direct aggression. No singeing of Hitler's moustache for the girls.

A twelve year old told her MO questioner on 27 April 1940 of a dream she'd just had which, in many ways, is a classical anxiety dream – being on display yet frozen, nearly paralysed and totally unable to perform an act one is ordinarily able to carry out easily:

> It's funny you should ask me [what she thought of the war]. Because I had a dream all about Hitler that night. It wasn't a political dream or anything, but it was funny. I dreamt that I saw a lot of people kneeling before Hitler; I knew it was only a dream, so I thought I'd cheek him. I was scared what he'd say. But he was ever so nice, and showed me all round the building. Then we came into a room full of grand pianos. I can play a bit, you see. So I tried to play 'Way Down Upon the Swannee River', but I couldn't find the notes. It was dreadful. I didn't know what he'd say. I woke up still looking for the notes.

While not many were as imaginative as this twelve year old, who conjured up Felliniesque dreams of rooms full of grand pianos on which she could not coax out a melody for a shadowy dictator, girls certainly appear to have dwelt less on death and destruction than boys, and tended instead to focus more on the war's side-effects and limitations. For example, one unnamed girl, aged eleven, detested evacuation, as she confessed to the MO reporter:

> The greatest change the war has made is evacuation. I think it's a horrible idea. The black-out is not at all bad; I think it's

rather fun going in the dark. I think we're fighting for a good purpose because if Hitler got all Europe, as he would like to, no one would be happy or have any peace. I think Hitler is a selfish old pig who only thinks of himself, and thinks he's marvellous and wants to boss everybody about and get the whole world for himself.

It is also obvious that evacuation was greeted with hostility by children especially close to their mothers. They certainly remarked on the 'rationed' visiting. To the reporter's query as to why she hadn't been evacuated, eleven-year-old Betty replied:

I went away but it wasn't very nice – they never treated me right, so I come back. I'm glad to be back. I didn't half miss them [her parents]. I'd never go away again. My mother said she would never send me away again. She only came down once the whole time I was there – I didn't half miss her.

Katie, aged thirteen, had been sent away to two, different, rural billets and, like Betty, blessed the day she'd been returned. She announced:

The war's nasty, driving you away from your own home and you can't settle down. I've been evacuated for two years to Northampton and Devon. I don't like to leave my parents because I'm happy with them.

Both boys and girls had reservations about certain aspects of the war. Rationing constituted a serious inroad into pleasure. As one boy of ten told a reporter, 'War's a nuisance, all the sweets are on coupons now.' The same investigator heard one eight-year-old girl, at a party, refuse chocolates then add, 'I mustn't take your rations.' He attributed her refined refusal, with its patriotic overtone to a direct copy of maternal behaviour, and he may have been right.

The war's capacity to create family disruption disturbed many young girls, as the MO reporter noted in her interpretation of the children's comments. It broke up families – it also destroyed lives, as another serious fourteen-year-old, Betty, was able to understand:

War is a waste of time and loss of life. All your uncles and brothers are called away and have to join up; maybe your father has to go abroad, and if he gets killed you'd never forgive the other people.

Wendy, aged eleven, whom the MO observer described as 'the youngest of four children, and rather spoiled and inconsequent', echoed feminine distaste for the savagery of war:

OBSERVER: What is your opinion about the war?

WENDY: I don't know. It's a horrid old war.

OBSERVER: What's wrong with it?

WENDY: All this killing. It isn't right to kill.

OBSERVER: What else don't you like about it?

WENDY: Having to carry my gas mask about with me.

OBSERVER: Why? Is it such a bother?

WENDY: Yes, I should jolly well think it is.

OBSERVER: Do your friends think so, too?

WENDY: Yes, you should hear what they have to say about it at school. And air-raid practices, I don't like them.

OBSERVER: Will you be glad when it's all over?

WENDY: Yes, they should stop it now.

OBSERVER: How?

WENDY: Just stop it.

Even patriotic fervour did not manage to convince most children of the value of gas masks and air-raid drills. The tight feel of latex over the face struck many of them as claustrophobic. Bobby, eleven, said he hated school and lessons, and told the MO reporter that he detested air-raid practice just as much as reading and writing, because he had to wear his gas mask which smelt 'all rubbery and nasty'.*

Grown-ups, who were children in World War II, still remember gas masks as one of the most onerous aspects of the struggle and would corroborate Bobby's opinion of them. Pauline Shaw, a retired Granada TV producer and director, aged fifteen in 1939, remembers the very outbreak of war because her stern Mancunian father ordered her to take her gas mask with her when she went out to join a gang of friends in a park in suburban Manchester. She had been frightened of what the gas mask represented – protection in

*Most of the schoolchildren questioned in 1940 attended the Dempsey Street school in Stepney which no longer exists.

case of enemy attack – and felt her worst fears were about to be realized. She related her wartime fears recently to me at her home in Hove, Sussex:

> It was Sunday, the 3rd of September, and Father had been listening to Chamberlain declaring war on the radio. He looked very serious. Later, when I said I was going out to meet my chums in the park, he reprimanded me for trying to dash out without wearing my gas mask around my neck. I refused initially, so we had a row. But he insisted and was more stern than I could ever remember him being. He reduced me to tears. I suppose he was worried about the war and it all got channelled into this confrontation with me. We could both be stubborn. But the upshot of all this is that I remember one of the most historic moments in my life because of the blazing row with my father more than the event itself. Now I realize that part of the reason for my tears was fear of what was to come.

Though air-raid practice and gas masks received the thumbs-down from the majority of children in 1940, many of them would have conceded that war had its bright moments with irregular school attendance topping the list. If an inchoate wish for peace did creep into some of the schoolchildren's consciousness, it often resulted from a vague idea that peace would bring back much-prized material comfort. For Frank, aged nine: 'A war is terrible – it means killing people and thousands called away from their homes, while peace means luxuries and pleasures.'

While the early stages of the war did bring severe shortages of childhood goodies such as ice cream, biscuits, gooey desserts and chocolates, which were soon replaced by carrot marmalade, crumbles made with stale bread, lashings of reconstituted dried eggs, margarine (and not much of it) instead of butter, and other types of dreary, though nutritious fare, the shops continued doing a brisk business in toys, especially during Christmas 1939, and even a year later in 1940. As the MO investigators discovered, toys and board-games reflected the public's interest in the war or, more precisely, manufacturers were keenly aware that children, especially boys, were obsessed by it and rushed in with a, now familiar, commercial urgency to satisfy their preoccupation. No doubt parents were as dismayed then as they are now at this unholy alliance between child and manufacturer, but all the same it proved a profitable union for some.

The MO observers cased the department stores in London before Christmas 1940, and wrote that the season 'has seen the advent of a spate of toys and games associated in one way or another with a state of war'. They looked at the toy departments of Harrods, Marks & Spencer and Woolworth's. Harrods, then as now, had one of the most variegated selections of toys, and the battle theme was strongly present with lead soldiers, uniformed dolls, tanks, searchlights and aeroplanes much in evidence. Marks & Spencer was supplying child-sized replicas of popular uniforms of the Services, and Woolworth's at Notting Hill Gate had displays of jigsaws with twelve motifs, four of which referred to the war – all designs connected with the army and anti-aircraft defences.

Cartoon strips were also adding gently to the war fever, according to MO. Out of numerous editions of *Beano* displayed in the week 2–9 March 1940, three strips carried war references – a joke about sergeants, one about scuttling and the last about escaped Nazi prisoners. Other cartoon strips examined that week were *Chips*, which had a long story about U-boats, and *Golden*, which featured a story about an air-ace and his swashbuckling encounters in mid-air with the enemy. Some boys' magazines for the over-tens were heavily influenced by the war, too. These were *Wizard*, *Skipper*, *Champion* and *Rover*; 12 per cent of their contents dealt with the Services, as opposed to a tiny percentage given over to jokes and pets, topics normally given much attention in the boys' magazines in peacetime.

The war, ineluctably, entered into the children's games, again predominantly amongst the boys. The war-games the boys devised, described in detail by MO, were intensely imaginative and reveal their obsession with contemporary events. If they weren't reading about, or listening to, descriptions of the highlights of the war themselves – Dunkirk and the Battle of Britain were favourite topics* – they appeared to pick up information about them from their older brothers, uncles or fathers.

*Both Dunkirk, the successful evacuation of British forces from France, which took place between 27 May and 4 June 1940 and the Battle of Britain, which began on 10 July 1940 and did not finish until the end of October, were defensive rather than offensive actions, but they contained dashing examples of great valour and cunning, elements which appealed enormously to young boys. Churchill expressed it best when he spoke of Dunkirk in the House of Commons on 4 June: 'Wars are not won by evacuations. But there was a victory inside this deliverance, which should be noted. It was gained by the Air Force.'

(Later on in the war, the boys' games were inspired by the captives of Colditz and the Burma campaign.)

Three of the most popular games with the boys were 'Concentration Camps' (yes, but not the ones the phrase brings to mind today), 'Convoys' and 'Bombings'. The game of 'Concentration Camps' invariably took place around the railings of a church. As young Bert explained to MO:

We play it outside the church because it has got railings, and we pretend it's barbed wire. Some of us are the Nazi guards. We've been taken prisoner, and they search us for the secret plans, but they don't know that we've made a lot of different plans; only one of them is real. The rest are only fluff, in case some of our own men turn against us. We try to surround the concentration camp and get our boys away. We slosh the guards and pinch their clothes, and then we get our own men free. We got the idea from the pictures.

The game of 'Convoys' required at least six boys to line up, with one boy standing apart. The smallest boy stood at the start of the line, the tallest last. They all crouched down while the odd one out held up a handkerchief, tied up at one end, filled with sand. The boys crawled, crouching in a crocodile line until the one holding the sand-filled handkerchief hurled it into the air. If the sand 'bomb' fell on or near one of the boys, this eliminated him from the game. Boys tried to play the game in dead silence, pretending they were lorries in a convoy carrying ammunition.

'Bombings' was a more rudimentary game with a hint of delinquency about it. It entailed lifting a quart bottle of milk from a neighbour's doorstep and 'bombing' it to smithereens with bricks. (At the time of the launching of his autobiographical film, *Hope and Glory*, film director John Boorman told a TV interviewer that 'children are natural anarchists'. Both the game of 'Bombings' and some of the boyish shenanigans he portrays in his fine film, where the boys have a hilarious time hurling bomb rubble about after raids, would seem to prove his point about joyful anarchy.)

But adults at the end of 1940 did not think the war was very amusing, though their children might enjoy playing in its debris. In fact, after the particularly savage blitz of 7 September 1940 when, as Prince Charles has said, 'the Messerschmitts left only rubble', a large number of grown-ups began to panic. They grabbed their children and ran. This exodus was anything but orderly and the children and parents of this self-styled evacuation were called 'trekkers'.

5

The 'Trickle' Evacuation: The Trekkers

From the summer of 1940 onwards, families in the cities must have wondered why they ever felt cheated or bored by the 'Phoney War'. The real article had arrived and it was merciless and terrifying.

On 16 August 1940, southern England was subjected to heavy raids involving 1720 Luftwaffe aircraft. A week later the Luftwaffe began raiding RAF installations in the London area, and Portsmouth was also attacked. And then, through a ghastly error in the third week of August, ten Luftwaffe night-bombers dropped their deadly cargos on the heart of London instead of the bomb storage depots east of the city at Thameshaven.

RAF bombers, giving as good as they got, retaliated by attacking Berlin for the first time on 25–6 August; twenty-nine of the pilots claimed to have hit Berlin (but these were messy, inaccurate raids, historians agree, damaging outlying civilian areas as well as military targets). Hitler promised savage retaliation for the RAF attack on Berlin, announcing that the British had 'dropped their bombs indiscriminately' on farms and villages as well as military installations. 'We shall stop the handiwork of these night pilots,' he warned. And he made good his threat. On 7 September the Germans began their most savage raids on London with a force of 625 bombers directed against the capital. About 100 tons of explosives were dropped on London nearly every night until 13 November (with only ten days' let-up throughout this time).* All in all, the

*L. M. Bates describes this first day, 7 September, in the chapter entitled, 'The Thames on Fire' (from his book *The Battle of London River*): 'For a short time after Dunkirk [6 June 1940], there was a lull while the enemy force made new dispositions in the occupied countries . . . On 7th October, 1940, on a fine Saturday afternoon the major attack on this country began when some thousand enemy aircraft struck at the Thames and docks of

Germans flew 12,000 night sorties during this nine-week period.

And then, on 14 November, they decided to show what they could do to a provincial town and flattened Coventry, a blitz so total and brutal that the beautiful cathedral town has earned an entry in the military dictionaries forever – when a town has been razed to the ground by bombs, it is said to be 'Coventrated'. The town was small (its population 213,000, according to a 1938 survey), thus nearly everyone was involved in the ten-hour bombing: 554 people were killed, 865 wounded. An MO report concluded that the small size of the place caused its citizens to believe that 'Coventry is finished' and indeed the destruction was colossal; a hundred acres of the city's heart were destroyed and one-third of the houses rendered uninhabitable. An MO observer commented that the first reaction of the survivors was, not unnaturally, to think of escape; a 'let's-get-out-of-here-altogether' compulsion gripped everyone.

In the second phase of the war, which began in August 1940 and continued almost without respite until 1945 (in 1943, for example, when the civilian population thought the worst of the bombing was over, they were then harrowed by V-1 bombs, the 'doodlebugs', which had a surreal awfulness almost surpassing the other more 'conventional' bombs), the urge to flee the attacks and find appropriate shelter prevailed. This overwhelming desire, which cannot truly be described as hysteria or panic because it had a real cause, created the phenomenon called 'trekking'. Trekking of course meant walking and it also meant taking your child or children by the hand, removing your family from the site of a direct bomb hit, and finding refuge elsewhere. Trekking was not always effected by walking; many families simply piled into their cars and drove blindly into the countryside, or onto moors, depending on where they were. Angus Calder writes that trekking 'reflected the same, not irrational, instinct of self-preservation which had captured the London tubes for the people'. Historians such as Calder today and Titmuss in the 40s are anxious to stress that the phenomenon was governed more by an instinct of self-preservation than blind panic or cowardice, and this distinction seems a fair one. Parents, in particular, held a ferocious belief that their children had a right to live.

And it was becoming evident in the early 40s that the bombers were no respecters of either gender or age. Frances Faviell,

London. Goering told Germany on that day: "This is the historic hour when our air force for the first time delivered its stroke right into the enemy's heart."'

apparently a volunteer helper with war refugees, wrote this eye-witness account of the bombing of the Church of the Holy Redeemer in Chelsea, on 14 September 1940, published recently in a collection of riveting, off-the-cuff, contemporary reminiscences in *Reportage*:

> The Church of the Holy Redeemer is a massive building and I had been there several times to see the shelter in the crypt because some of our refugees liked this shelter so much that they wanted to change to it . . . It was a popular shelter – perhaps because, like the refugees, others felt that nowhere would they be safer than under the protection of the Church – and at the time the bomb fell it was crowded . . . The bomb had struck the Church at an angle, through a window, in a most extraordinary way and had penetrated the floor and burst among the shelterers, mostly women and small children . . . A woman who was in the shelter told me about it when I visited her afterwards in St Luke's Hospital. She was badly injured and said that the scene had resembled a massacre – in fact, she compared it to an engraving she had seen of the massacre of the women and children in Cawnpore in the Indian Mutiny, with bodies, limbs, blood, and flesh mingled with little hats, coats, and shoes and all the small necessities which people took to the shelter with them . . .

Such horrific killing of women and children changed the entire character of the evacuation process itself. Whereas in September 1939 evacuation had been a reasonably ordered affair overseen by the government, with train timetables and school parties carefully arranged, the Second Evacuation, which began a year later in September 1940, was much more *ad hoc*. Individuals began to organize their own evacuation, sometimes seeking partial help from the government (this was referred to as the 'assisted private evacuation scheme'). This new scheme started in June 1940, and it meant the government gave billeting and travel assistance to those who could find their own accommodation. The assisted scheme was necessary because bombing raids had begun to make any central overseeing on the government's part totally unfeasible.

The Second Evacuation took place throughout the United Kingdom. Towns that had been considered 'safe' became unsafe overnight, and coastal ports – such as Plymouth, Southampton, Swansea and Barrow – joined London as primary targets. Heavy raids on the Glasgow and Clydeside districts led Scottish parents to seize upon the assisted evacuation scheme; nearly 90 per cent of Scottish mothers and children became part of it and were billeted in regional reception districts, often in the far north of Scotland. As the safe areas in mainland Britain became more scarce, women and children began evacuating themselves to Northern Ireland and Eire. The rapidity with which so-called safe areas for evacuees became high-voltage danger zones was the primary reason that evacuation became a semi-private rather than a public affair.

The Welsh poet, Bryn Griffiths, described Swansea's changing wartime character, in lyrical fashion, in *Evacuees*:

I was born in Swansea, and grew up in a street near the docks, in squalor and poverty, one of the thousand slum children who played by the rust-coloured River Tawe, climbed the quarries of Kilvey Hill, and mitched, morning after morning, along the shores of Swansea Bay – staked and barb-wired then – while seagulls wheeled and sang harshly above our uncaring heads. We were poor, and dishonest, but life had colour and vitality.

And then the war came, almost unnoticed, with a few occasional air-raids, a splatter of bombs bursting harmlessly in the bay, and faraway dogfighting planes sketching a trellis of smoke-trails against the blue summer skies. It all seemed rather distant, peripheral, not really concerning us. We practised our air-raid drills, donned gas masks and laughed ourselves sick at the sight of friends suddenly turned into goggle-eyed goblins. It was as good as playing.

But then the war really came home to us. Three nights of devastating *blitzkrieg* smashed the docks, set Llandarcy refinery alight, and flattened nearly a square mile of Swansea. The town was torn apart, and hundreds killed, but only then did the local authorities decide to evacuate the town's children to the safer and less industrial areas of Wales.

So here I was, travelling; the Swansea dockland already becoming a memory as we trundled westwards to steam and shudder at last into Cardigan station.

Young Bryn Griffiths, forced to flee his Welsh coastal city after an unprecedentedly savage blitzkrieg, was a small player in what had become a vast drama staged by the German Luftwaffe. By the spring of 1941, the German militarists had established a new bombing pattern. Their strategists decided to direct their attacks principally against western ports feeding supplies to Britain from the sea. This resulted in sixty-one raids taking place in the twelve weeks from 19 February to 12 May 1941, including the 'Coventration' of Plymouth, followed by raids on other coastal towns, less savage, but violent enough to compel residents to flee. The spring of 1941 saw a strange occurrence: the seaside towns rapidly became ghost towns. Towns reporting more than a 50 per cent fall in population included Clacton, Dover, Eastbourne, Folkestone, Margate and Southend.

The German's targets, however, seemed randomly chosen (Brighton, for example, which had been considered a haven in 1939, became another 'evacuable' area after suffering raids in the early spring of 1941). Evacuation had to become instantaneous, meeting danger as it arose and, as Titmuss writes, 'local safety-valves were to be provided in different parts of the country immediately a city was heavily attacked'.

The new flexibility of the government scheme, with its device of 'assisted' evacuation, meant that the Second Evacuation of 1940–1, diffused as it was, sparked off another great wave of mothers and children leaving the inland cities and coastal towns for safer areas. Since this evacuation did not occur on one amazing day, as had the evacuation of 1 September 1939, it was dubbed the 'trickle' evacuation though, as statistics confirm, the 'trickles' often could more accurately be described as 'floods'. Titmuss reports:

> After a hesitant start in the autumn of 1940, the Government's evacuation policy developed a flexibility which allowed it to meet most of the demands for dispersal during 1941. Its achievements, in a purely numerical sense, may be summed up in a few figures.
>
> From September 1940 to the end of 1941, the total number of mothers and children sent away in organised parties from all evacuation areas in Britain to pre-arranged destinations was probably in the neighbourhood of 350,000 to 400,000: in this total there were about 141,000 unaccompanied children (129,000 from evacuation areas in England and Wales and 12,000 in Scotland). In addition, some 20,700 expectant mothers were evacuated under the special maternity scheme; 9,400 from London and 11,300 from other towns and cities . . . the total number of people in Britain who in this period were helped in some form or another by the Government to leave the bombed cities thus amounted to approximately 1,250,000.

Naturally, from the tidiness of Titmuss's writing and the concise-ness of his statistics, one can derive little, if any, knowledge of the real trauma suffered by those who were involved in this gigantic upheaval. It is difficult to imagine the barely muted panic that overtook a mother in the bombed cities when she no longer thought her in-house, Morrison shelter would prevent her children from being killed. (Mothers who didn't shelter in the tubes or in Anderson shelters in their back gardens, used the Morrison shelter. It was the brain-child of Herbert Morrison, former chief of the Labour-controlled London County Council, whom Churchill appointed as Home Secretary in the winter of 1940. Little more than a reinforced table, although it did provide shelter against flying shrapnel, it was no real protection against a direct hit. Its chief attraction was that it did mean a family could shelter in the relative warmth of their own homes. However, judging from the huge crowds which continued to gather in the underground to sleep overnight, faith in the Morrison shelter was not rock-solid.)

Betty Pooley, a 77-year-old widow and retired postal clerk who lived in Camberwell, South London, was a 31-year-old mother of two small children during the 1941 blitz.* She remembered how her initial faith in her reinforced table evaporated under a rain of bombs, which fell on the Elephant and Castle area from September 1940 until May 1941. Her husband, who had been an attendant at the Walworth Road baths, was in the forces and stationed in York. She and her two sons, Allen, three, and Harry, six, had been sheltering in the crypt of St Peter's Church in Walworth Road. During the spring, however, her sons simultaneously contracted chickenpox; she had to keep them at home and relied on her Morrison shelter in the hallway of her ground floor flat. Her escalating panic finally made her flee, to become what the officials might have called a 'private evacuee', or 'assisted' one. From her local council she got the train fare to Yorkshire for herself, her two boys and her ageing mother Emily, in her late sixties, but for all that her flight was not really planned. Except for the fact that she took a train instead of walking, she could also be described as a 'trekker'. Her whole being was concentrated on flight – 'We're going to get out of this and get out of it together' – was her motto, she said.

*I interviewed Betty Pooley in the autumn of 1986; we had been colleagues on the *Daily Express* and the best of office friends. She always said – prophetically, as it turns out – that I would 'tell her story' one day. She died in 1987.

I had the table in the hallway and the boys sleeping under it, both sporting their rashes. I was worried about not being able to take them to the crypt that week but they were feverish and it just wasn't on. The shrapnel would come down and it looked like big lumps of rusted iron. These big lumps would pound the front door and make the doorbell ring, and I'd keep going to the door thinking there was someone there out on the step and, of course, it would be shrapnel falling.

Then one night, this big bomb came down and hit the crypt. Anyone available dashed out to see if they could help. One whole family of six got killed. My older brother was a volunteer worker and he joined the rescuers. When the bomb dropped, our whole house rocked. It was terrifying. I felt it was fateful that my kids had chickenpox and so we weren't in the crypt that night. But I felt no fear. When you have young children, you tend to forget about yourself. An official evacuation of mothers and children was being organized, but I wouldn't wait. I had previously applied for some train fare from the Council and I had received it, so I just decided to go then and there. I collected my mother, Emily, a real darling, and headed for King's Cross station. I had some vague idea that I should try to get to Yorkshire because my husband was stationed there, but it wasn't very carefully thought out. I just knew that the four of us had to be together – Emily, the boys, and me – and that we had to get away from Walworth Road.

I went to collect my mother, took the boys to say goodbye to their grandfather – he didn't want to join us because he felt his duty lay in staying there, I suppose. We then high-tailed it over to King's Cross station and I've never seen such chaos and confusion with queues of mothers and children everywhere. Looking back, I think I developed some queer kind of amnesia or something, because I can't remember much except saying 'Be quiet or else!' to the boys, and then I think I attached myself to what was probably an official line of evacuating mothers and children, but at that point I don't think I cared about being unofficial. I just attached myself to the line and prayed. It worked. No one prevented us from getting on the train.

Then it all seems a dream and I lost track of time but we did end up at a place called Poppyton in Yorkshire. We were e chosen by country people – maybe it was because

I kept saying – 'Does anyone have a cottage?' I didn't want to be billeted where I'd have to share. The miracle is that someone *did* have a gardener's cottage on an estate. The gardener had been called up, the lady of the manor explained. She took us to the cottage in a chauffeur-driven limousine and was wonderful to us, getting her maids to clean up the place and make the beds and so on. But she never interfered – never came knocking on the door afterwards, but would do kind things, like giving my sons six eggs a week to bring back to me.

Betty Pooley learned to love the countryside, especially its wild flowers, although like a homing pigeon, she returned to spend her remaining years on the Walworth Road. Old habits die hard. Her mother, who died some years before her, never fully adjusted to the tranquillity of her Yorkshire refuge:

One day I found mother walking around the garden in Poppyton with her gas mask on. I asked her what on earth she thought she was doing wearing a gas mask in a country garden and she pointed at the morning mist. She thought it was bomb smoke!

I could do some very citified things, too. I was unused to harmless insects. One day I saw the cottage door was covered with them – greenfly, or midges perhaps – and I doused the door with disinfectant. Our landlady thought I was a bit daft, I think. But she was very sweet about it.

In fact, my landlady was wonderful in every way. I had become pregnant before I left London, and I soon knew for certain by the time we were billeted in the cottage. But I kept quiet about it, thinking we might be moved out with one more child on the way. But when I went into labour, the landlady called a doctor and was very comforting. I gave birth to David, my third son, but he was a spina bifida baby and died a few days after his birth. He is buried in Poppyton at All Saints Church.

After the funeral, the vicar was lovely and kept reminding me that I still had two beautiful boys. But I keep wondering even now, if my baby might not have lived if it hadn't have been for the bombings and all the confusion of fleeing London. I know he was handicapped but I still regret his death and think it might have been avoided.

Betty Pooley confessed to always feeling a slight twinge of guilt at having 'conned herself' out of London by unofficially joining an official line of evacuating mothers and children during that week after her own church-crypt shelter had sustained a direct hit. But she needn't have; countless mothers like her 'headed out' with just as much determination. Bureaucratic red tape could not stop them: some merely grabbed their train fare and ran, leaving their belongings behind.

Frank R. Lewey, the mayor of Stepney, described the chaos in 1940 as mothers and babies 'scrambled' to the train stations for points west and north. As he relates in *The Home Front*:

> We resolved to occupy the People's Palace, the theatre in the Mile End Road where I had listened to opera while the first bombs fell. This place was big enough to give us elbow-room in handling the masses of homeless who were already tramping in like a retreating army, seeking our assistance . . .
>
> When we first set up business at the People's Palace . . . our very first task was to arrange for the evacuation of mothers and small children who had been rendered homeless, and, after those, for mothers and children who wished to get out of London . . .
>
> I see myself, dog-tired after a terrific day's work, dragging wearily out of the People's Palace and seeing in front of me a great area of deserted prams in the evening light, with the drifting smoke of nearby burning houses dimming them . . . The mothers had brought their babies in prams – and, of course, we had not foreseen that – and, as they could not take the prams with them on the overcrowded trains, they just had to leave them there in front of the building, so that it was, by evening, hardly possible to get in or out except by climbing over a great expanse of them . . .

Some mothers relied, chaotically, on the help of officialdom. Others cast any form of state or local civic help aside, listening only to their own premonitions, however shadowy or inexplicable. In the panic that the nightly bombings instilled, there arose a great faith, not always in the Almighty – whose places of worship, in any case, were receiving a pasting – but in intuition or alternative sources of guidance. For instance, the MO discovered that astrology columns in newspapers were becoming highly popular. Their readership rose by 30 per cent, while no corresponding rise in church attendance or religious observance was reported.

Ethel Salmon, fifty, Harry Salmon's wife,* only dimly remembers her mother's quixotic behaviour when the bombs were dropping over Canning Town, East London, when she was three years old. She is now unsure whether her memory of her mother's unceremonious bundling of herself, her brothers and her sisters out of the city has come to her through family mythology, or whether she does really recall the dramatic exodus itself.

The authorities told us we should shelter at the local school, but Mother didn't care for this idea as the bombs kept coming down – it was late September 1940, I think, when they got bad. Anyway, she had a premonition that the school would be unsafe and so she decided to act alone and quickly. She got hold of a leg of lamb from the butcher, and took the five of us to Bury St Edmunds in Suffolk. She held me in one arm and the leg of lamb in the other.

Because she was an unofficial evacuee, she was stranded when she got there, after getting out at the station. But we got help in the shape of the local vicar, thank heavens, who arranged for us to stay in a dilapidated thatched cottage. The whole family still discusses the size of the spiders there – you just couldn't kill them!

We stayed in the cottage for two years but we were never accepted by the villagers. No one would entertain the Londoners. Father was with us and he kept urging mother to return to Canning Town. When we did get back, our house was demolished, but Dad did up our bombed building.

We later found out that, the day Mother took us off to Suffolk, the school building in Canning Town was bombed – the one we were supposed to have used as a shelter. It was flattened completely and 300 mothers and children were killed.

Ethel Salmon blinks back tears when she remembers her mother's quirky, but accurate, premonition. A sensible, no-nonsense mother of a grown-up son and two daughters, and also a grandmother of two, Ethel works tirelessly in her husband's prosperous off-licence, and lays no claim to a belief in the supernatural. Still, she admits to respecting the intuitive feelings of her late mother.

*See Harry Salmon, Chapter 4, pp. 58–9.

Like many other evacuees, Ethel derived an abiding love of the country from her long-ago sojourn in the spider-infested thatched cottage and delights in pruning her rose garden, bordering Epping Forest, and picnicking at weekends in Laindon, Essex, with her children and grandchildren. Unlike Harry, the blanket silence of a country lane does not give her the shudders. Ethel affirms that her family were never accepted nor absorbed into the community in their adopted village near Bury St Edmunds in 1940, but possibly this resulted from her parents' own self-sufficiency and pride, a policy of keeping to themselves and asking no favours.

The signs were, however, that during the Second Evacuation the 'tricklers' or 'trekkers', whatever one chooses to call them, were tolerated a great deal more in the country than they were during the First 'Phoney War' Evacuation in 1939. The presence of real danger in the cities, the fact that the evacuees, accompanied or unaccompanied by their parents, were actually running for their lives, swayed people in the reception centres, forcing them to display hospitality and an emotional flexibility that they had not previously possessed. Billeters and responsible school heads, delegated by local authorities to oversee the welfare of evacuees in homes and hostels, almost developed rictus smiles in their effort to think positively about their charges. It was not always easy. Southampton schoolmaster, Eric Wyeth Gadd, made the following irritable entries in his diary on 3 January 1941, concerning young teenage refugees in his care, at a hostel at Furzie Close. He could barely conceal his outrage:

1. Within a few hours of their arrival a number of the younger members of the party broke into the fowlhouse and killed the fowls, which were consumed by some of the F.C. guests. The police were called in.

2. Contrary to instructions, their people light fires in the wards and cook what they fancy there.

3. Most of the men come in drunk each night. At Christmas the doctor was called in to deal with a number of boys of 12 and 13 who had been sick: he pronounced them drunk.

Nonetheless Gadd, while flaying his young, yobbish 'unbilletables', as he called them, and praising the Women's Voluntary Services' volunteers, who scrubbed and cooked for them (thanklessly, it appears), forced himself to look on 'the bright side'. In

fact, he titled one chapter of his diary, recounting events in
1940, 'The Brighter Side', and apologetically prefaced it with these
words:

> The preceding chapter may suggest that the whole evacuation
> scene was littered with difficult problems. Far from it. As every
> wise newspaper reader knows, good news is often no news: in
> the same way, smooth running seldom provides material for a
> diary. However, the following may help to redress the
> balance . . .

He goes on to describe one family and their luminously happy
evacuee charges, in an entry written on 21 July 1940:

> This evening visited the home of Mrs Keatley who, in a tiny
> cottage, billets five children aged between seven and twelve.
> Welcomed by cry of greeting from bedroom window, where
> children, in nightclothes, were waiting for prayers. My teasing
> suggestion that they should all be sent home was greeted by a
> unanimous 'No, Sir!' The obvious happiness of these children
> may well mean uneasy problems when the time comes for them
> to return home. And this contentment is in spite of (or because
> of?) very firm handling: eg. the sitting room is the 'holy of
> holies', where the children are allowed on only special oc-
> casions; each child has duties which are compulsory (such as
> washing up and drying); when 'Uncle' comes home from work
> 'Auntie' will not attend to children's problems. The secrets of
> success seem to be fairness, firmness and well-directed activity.
> On one occasion Ray (twelve) was only forgiven for refusal to
> dry the dishes as a result of persistent pleading from Joan
> (twelve) and Jean (eight); he has never since refused – now
> often asks for the task. Joan sums it all up: 'Auntie's the best
> one in Ashley!'

That Mr and Mrs Keatley were running a very tidy ship with
their five evacuee charges, overseen by the delighted Mr Gadd, is
undeniable. One wonders if the natural parents, visiting their
children and seeing them so strictly, if amicably, disciplined, might
not have felt pangs of jealousy at their altered behaviour. It must
have been difficult not to be afflicted by envy, on occasion, at the
sight of such even-tempered and structured familial harmony.

However, foster-parents had been given *carte blanche* to act *in loco*

*parentis** by the Ministry of Health, which adjudicated in these
matters. The evacuees' surrogate parents could be as bossy as they
liked in the interests of maintaining order: they were acting within
their rights. At times, this situation must have been galling for
the children's rightful parents, alone, and threatened nightly with
possible annihilation in the cities. Their only redress, as we know,
was to recall their children, something that was done with regularity
in 1939. In the Second Evacuation the children were still recalled,
but in smaller numbers. To bring a child home to the danger
zones now seemed as capricious and irresponsible as the chiding
government posters constantly suggested. Even to have a child
home for a holiday was discouraged. As Gadd writes in a 14
March 1942 diary entry: 'Today we have sent to the parents of all
Southampton children a strongly-worded letter urging against the
recall of evacuees at Easter.'

Southampton's suburbs were dubious places of safety for evacuated children, as Gadd's diary proves, but by July 1941, enemy
action had badly damaged its schools and daily raids rendered it
'evacuable' shortly afterwards. Gadd announced: 'From 1st October
until 18th November warnings are recorded almost daily.' In exas-
peration, he reported that 'more than nineteen hours of schooling'
were lost through warnings between the 10th July and December
1940. The evacuation of Southampton started after he wrote this
cryptic entry: 'Dec. 2 – Terrible damage was done during the
week-end by enemy action – School unfit for use – Many evacuated.'
On 3 December he records: 'No school – Teachers preparing lists
of children for evacuation ... Dec. 7th – The Headmaster with
other escorts took 125 ch: to Dorchester and Beaminster. The
Northam evacuees numbered twelve (boys).'

Hearing that this group of schoolboys was going to be evacuated
to Beaminster, one of Gadd's school-cleaners put down her broom
and bucket and snorted: 'What do they want to go to that horrible
place for?' A saucy kind of civic pride existed in many townspeople's

---

*As the Ministry of Health's *Memo. Ev. 4*, printed by HMSO in 1939, states in Clause
72: 'In the circumstances in which evacuation would take place, householders in the receiving
areas could be relied on to do everything possible to lighten the lot of the children and
mothers compelled suddenly to leave their homes and families and finding themselves in
strange surroundings. So far as unaccompanied schoolchildren are concerned, the house-
holder will be *in loco parentis*, and should have no great difficulty in controlling the children
and preserving reasonable discipline. The children will be accompanied by their teachers,
who will know them and will be able to assist in their control.'

minds, and watching their homes and schools bombed to smithereens only increased their pride in their stricken towns.

Other coastal towns were faring no better and plans for their
evacuation were cobbled together as speedily as in Southampton.
Dover had come to be called 'Hell's Corner' because of its proximity
to Occupied France, its niche in history as the landing-place in
June 1940 of the ragged survivors of Dunkirk, and the unenviable
vulnerability of its harbour to constant German bombing raids.
According to Frank Illingworth, a journalist, it was not a happy
place for animals, either. He had co-operated with the police in
dealing with 176 dogs which had returned from Dunkirk with the
troops; the majority of the dogs had to be destroyed. He described
the sad farrago of animals, children, troops and refugees from
Dunkirk, that mingled in the streets of Dover in June 1940:

> Many animals accompanied Dover children in the evacuation
> trains. The first batch of children left us on June 2, 1940. It
> was a sad Sunday. Men (and dogs) were still arriving from
> Dunkirk; the town was still sprinkled with French, Dutch and
> Belgian soldiers and sailors; there were a few civilian refugees
> – possessing little more than the clothes they wore – who had
> somehow managed to scramble aboard British ships; one little
> girl, whose mother had been killed by a marauding German
> fighter plane, was carried on to the platform on a stretcher,
> wounded in the arm.
>
> Through this atmosphere, heavy with tension, Dover chil-
> dren marched to the Priory Station. Few parents accompanied
> them: good-byes had been completed at home, and the chil-
> dren, though obviously bewildered, stood up to the occasion
> manfully. They were bound for Wales.

Eye-witness accounts of the raids on the coastal towns in 1940
show that the civilians, although terrified of the bombs, were eerily
fascinated by the machinery of war unleashed before their eyes.
'Nearly everyone in those roads,' wrote one Portsmouth resident of
the neighbourhood surrounding the harbour, 'used to watch in those
early days – never went to a shelter.' He breathlessly delineated the
events of 12 August; his words are recorded in a local history
manual, *Portsmouth at War*:

> At about 12 o'clock I passed a sailor, riding a bicycle painted
> yellow and sounding a bugle. This was the Yellow Warning:

the Air Raid Precaution people being alerted to a likely attack. Then the sirens began to wail, meaning it was a red warning and attack was imminent. Then after that, all I can say is, all hell was let loose. The next half hour was the noisiest I have ever known in my life. All the heavy guns were firing, the planes were screaming down because it was a dive bombing attack, and the pompoms on the warships in harbour opened up . . . I do remember hearing the bombs whistle down. My first reaction was: 'Oh – they do whistle after all.' Often I'd been to films where I'd heard whistling when bombs were falling, but people said to me they'd made it up . . . When it was all over and eventually the all clear went, I cycled off home to lunch. When I went out of the main gate, I saw that the shelter in St George's Square had received a direct hit. I cycled up Park Road, and along the railways line and then the sirens went for another warning. In front of me there was a large sheet of water where a water main had been burst by a bomb hitting it, and I couldn't get through.

I remember there were a lot of very small children who must have been on their way home from school and had been stopped and then let go again when the all-clear went. They were terrified because they couldn't get across the road because of the water.

The fact that German bombs were now falling directly onto shelters and schools was a powerful incentive for parents (even those who had previously sworn they would never be parted from their children) to see that their children were evacuated in 'trickles' to Dorset, Wales and other safer areas in the southwest.

Meanwhile, London's East Enders were harrowed nightly throughout the autumn of 1940 (except for 2 November – weather conditions prevented the German bombers from making raids.) The Docklands sustained horrific damage from the skies. According to Angus Calder:

Many East Enders lived virtually on islands, connected only by bridges with London's mainland. In the Surrey Docks, fires threatened the two bridges across which the 'local inhabitants' could escape. By heroic action, a thousand people, old and young, mothers and children, were evacuated.

One of the heroines was the local W.V.S. organizer, who collected a convoy of cars and, when these proved insufficient, appealed for anything on wheels; 'even the dustcarts', she added, 'and the dustcarts came'. In the following days, two other dock areas in a similar plight were evacuated; on the 9th, the town clerk of Stepney, entirely on his own initiative, arranged for a thousand people to be taken to safety in river steamers.

Bernard Kops,* then twelve, was trying to keep his spirits aloft in Bethnal Green, at the time, by riding the tube escalators with his younger sister, Phyllis. But their insouciance was difficult to maintain amid the sound of nightly sirens – 'sirens and sirens', as he put it; he regretted the loss of something far more precious than his youthful effervescent gaiety – to wit, his childhood:

> And we went underground to get away from the sirens and the bombs. Yet they followed me and I heard sirens until the world became a siren. One endless cry of torture. It penetrated right into the core of my being, night and day was one long night, one long nightmare, one long siren, one long wail of despair. Some people feel a certain nostalgia for those days, recall a poetic dream about the blitz. They talk about those days as if they were time of a true communal spirit. Not to me. It was the beginning of an era of utter terror, of fear and horror. I stopped being a child and came face to face with the new reality of the world.

Shortly after Bernard Kops realized he'd become an unwilling adult, Liverpool Street station and two other termini suffered direct hits, killing over three hundred people. Bernard was lucky that night because he and his sister, feeling naughty, had hopped on a tube train to the West End, unknowingly leaving death and carnage behind them. But these chilling events prompted his mother to decide to quit her beloved Bethnal Green, and head for Yorkshire and the bleak Dales she learned to know and hate.

The MO reporters tried to analyse why it was Mrs Kops and thousands like her were giving in to what MO termed 'unplanned hysteria'. One reporter was of the opinion that people were completely unprepared intellectually for the *extent* of the raid damage:

> While direct fear of death is naturally a factor of importance in causing people to leave, more important still would seem to

*See Chapter 2, pp. 31–2

The Reason Why: Air-raid warden holds a terrified
child after a V-1 attack, Buckingham Gate, London,
23 June 1944.

We Think You Have to Go: *(above)* Parents wave goodbye to their children at Blackhorse Road station, London, September 1939; *(centre)* Small girl examines the identification tag of her companion, London, 1940; *(below)* London evacuees with gas masks and luggage assembling at mainline station.

Class Distinctions and the Common Denominator: *(above left)* London urchin eating toffee carrot; *(above right)* Middle-class evacuees en route abroad; *(below)* Gas-mask tests for children at Kent nursery, 20 October 1937.

Happy Travellers: *(above)* Carriage windows crowded with children about to set off for the West Country from Paddington; *(below)* Evacuee children from London receiving refreshments on their way to safety.

Unhappy Arrivals: *(above)* London volunteer worker and inconsolable boy, wartime terminus, 23 May 1942; *(below)* Children in reception centre, London, ready for evacuation to the country, 1 May 1940.

Billeting: *(above left)* Billeting officer with children and foster-parents, 1939; *(above right)* London children being received by their new 'mother' at their billet in a small village in Surrey; *(below)* Evacuees at 'Fairlawns', home of Peter Cazalet, the trainer of racehorses belonging to the Queen Mother.

Town Meets Country: *(above)* Young evacuees out for a stroll with their teacher in a Berkshire village, 14 October 1940; *(below)* London children evacuated to Dorset gathering acorns.

Further Afield: *(above)* The ill-fated evacuee ship, *City of Benares*, sunk in mid-Atlantic, 17 September 1940; *(below)* Scottish 'Seavacs' celebrate their safe arrival in New York.

be the feeling of time-hopelessness. The feeling that these raids will now go on forever (every person interviewed on Monday expected the present state of affairs to continue, expected attacks to be concentrated on the East End) . . . Everything points to the noise as a major factor in causing severe tension and making resistance break at an early stage.

This observer was scornful of the press's attempt to present the East Enders as personifications of 'smiling jollity and fun'. He could detect no sign of humour, laughter or whistling. 'Here people wanted to be brave,' he wrote, 'but found bravery was something purely negative, cheerless, and without encouragement or prospect of success.' Many women shared this despondent East Ender's sentiments: 'I can't stand it. It's killing me. This ain't war, this is murder. It's absolutely killing me.'

Her sense of hopelessness was mirrored everywhere; a state of mind exacerbated by what MO called '*listening tension* . . . listening for the planes, listening for the bombs'. And the tension produced a 'resistance break', they reported, resulting in the spontaneous migration of hordes of people from Mile End, Whitechapel, Stepney and Bow to Oxford. MO found it a difficult migration to understand:

> The evacuation was done entirely without planning. Often those who are on the move expressed a sort of surprise at finding they were going. Plenty went without any plan at all, without any money or prospects. One definite stream developed towards Paddington and kept flowing there largely by imitation, turning into a migration for Oxford (at least it was followed until it had practically filled the available space on the 3:30 for Oxford).

The town of Oxford was not prepared for the influx of evacuees – mothers, fathers and children – who came in their thousands from the East End. In desperation, the city fathers commandeered the Majestic Cinema, originally meant to hold a maximum of 2000 cinema-goers, but which now became the foetid shelter for over three times that number. The atmosphere, with thousands of dazed and sleepy mothers stretching out on palliasses with their babies, fathers snoring into the night, and litter and nappies everywhere, was nightmarish. A movie was still being advertised outside, ironically titled *Babes in the Wood*, starring Mickey Rooney. Somehow milk and sandwiches were supplied for all, as well as blankets and steaming cups of hot, 'sergeant-major's' tea. The feat of catering for such a multitude was organized by the Public Assistance Department of the Oxford City Council with the town's Medical Officer of Health providing the nursing staff, and the WVS, the sandwich-makers.

Racial remarks were ugly and frequent at the Majestic: one refugee – and here the term 'refugee' can surely supplant 'evacuee', as this helter-skelter run to safety included as many adults as children – said that he objected to being treated like a foreigner, 'a nigger or Chinaman'. MO reported a nasty upsurge of anti-Semitic feeling as well. Many of the Majestic inmates thought 'rich Jews' could afford the Oxford hotels and bed-and-breakfast guest-houses, which they could not. No one was able to pinpoint the source of this rumour, nor confirm its accuracy; happily, this distressing outbreak of racial resentment subsided almost as quickly as it had arisen. Anti-Semitism became particularly unacceptable a few years later when Britons realized what outcome such sentiments had had in Germany.

Oxonians, though dazed by the invasion by the East Enders, rose magnificently to the occasion, householders absorbing mothers and children into billets wherever possible. Their compassion was aroused by the tales of horror, which circulated among the refugees, and they began to believe London, especially the East End, was little more than a mass of smoking ruins.

One, more customary, result of the catastrophic events was an upsurge in trading in the autumn of 1940 for Oxford shopkeepers. Business was brisk if unglamorous. As one trader told MO scornfully, 'I suppose it's good for trade but it's all scrap trade. Halfpenny sweets and penny novelties, they all go. Still it's all ready money and that's welcome these days.'

Despite the overcrowding and filth present at the Majestic (toilet facilities mirrored those of a congested prison), the temporary residents' health did not suffer; few physical diseases more alarming than an outbreak of boils were reported. Psychologically, the worst feature of life in this transformed cinema was boredom: the women had nothing to do and nowhere to go and the children no suitable way to work off their energies. One MO report stated that many of the young children just ran around and around, outside the Majestic building, like hamsters on wheels. As lighting was restricted to save electricity, the interior of the cinema was always gloomily lit; in the greenish half-light evacuation assumed the colours of a nightmarish

Hieronymus Bosch painting. Vera Brittain described this scene in her autobiography *England's Hour*. The fact that Oxford was the beloved university town where she had spent some of her happiest years, as an undergraduate, lend her reminiscences a special poignancy:

> Amongst the rugs and perambulators on the short dry grass [fronting the Majestic] lie pieces of chewed apple core, fragments of orange peel, and the inevitable sheets of torn dirty newspaper which indicate, like a paper trail, the presence of an evacuee population the moment that it moves from its normal environment.
>
> As I enter the cinema, a familiar and overpowering stench strikes me on the face like a blow. Where did I last encounter it? I wonder, and then I remember; it was the smell of the crowded Ladies' Saloon on the night boat during a rough Channel crossing. Gradually my nose becomes accustomed to it as my eyes also accommodate themselves to the unillumined twilight inside the building. Covering the floor beneath the upturned velveteen seats of the cinema chairs, disorderly piles of mattresses, pillows, rugs and cushions indicate the 'pitches' staked out by each evacuated family. Many of the women, too dispirited to move, still lie wearily on the floor with their children beside them in the foetid air, though the hour is 11 a.m. and a warm sun is shining cheerfully on the city streets. Between the mattresses and cushions, the customary collection of soiled newspapers and ancient apple-cores is contributing noticeably to the odoriferous atmosphere. A few small boys, evidently set to the task by the organisers on the floor above, are making a determined attack on the extensive squalor with besoms and brooms.

In spite of this malodorous and depressing picture, Vera Brittain's memoir does show that the Cockney spirit, one of feisty unsinkability, persisted. A mother from Poplar, rejecting any sympathetic displays from Miss Brittain, brought her up short by telling her that the tea served was 'just like dish-water'.

Vera Brittain's reaction of compassionate horror was genuinely felt. She sensed keenly the divide between the 'haves and have-nots'; the 'East End and West End' as she candidly wrote. Shortly after touring the Majestic, she was forced to evacuate her own two children, son John, and one of the most famous evacuees of all, daughter Shirley, later to become politician Shirley Williams. But her children did not sleep on the floor amid apple cores and litter in a benighted movie house. They were sent overseas to North America.

It is ironic that Vera Brittain, so aware of class divisions in the evacuation process, should have opted for what was a predominantly middle-class solution when considering the plight of her own children. However, few would blame a parent for choosing a more comfortable alternative than one involving chaos and squalor. A great many mothers and fathers, who could afford to do so, *did* choose a softer option for their children, but not always that of sending them overseas. Often, they sent them to boarding school or to friends in a safer zone. It was the middle-class way out.

6

The Middle-Class Exodus

If the East Enders were seen trekking blindly to the genteel environs of Oxford and other provincial towns during the terrifying 1940–1 Blitz on London, a more subtle, less visible, but nonetheless substantial exodus of the professional classes and their children was also taking place in London and elsewhere at that time. This middle-class exodus was greater than a 'trickle', but because it was not government-sponsored and monitored, exact figures of its extent were never obtained. However, many commentators put the figure at over two million people. As Constantine Fitzgibbon writes in his book, *The Blitz*:

> Another sort of evacuation was more successful [than the initial one of September 1939]. Something over two million people hurried out of London, under their own steam or in their own motor-cars, as soon as the war broke out. Many of them stayed away, and *The Times* was to write, in early 1941, of country hotels 'filled with well-to-do refugees, who too often have fled for nothing. They sit and read and knit and eat and drink . . .'
> A high proportion had already reserved accommodation for themselves in safe areas; others just locked up their London flats and drove off.

The middle-class evacuation was, like the official ones, subject to ebbs and flows; lonely parents recalled their children from the country when there was a lull in the bombing and then sent them off again when there was a savage renewal. Fee-paying London day schools such as Westminster, St Paul's and City of London, removed themselves *en bloc* to the country, usually installing themselves in the accommodation of another, already existing, school. As the war dragged on, some such schoolboys began to think of themselves

as belonging to their adoptive schools. My first husband, Keith
Woodeson, for example, was evacuated from the City of London
School in his early teens in 1940, to his home town school of Marlborough in Wiltshire; four years, and a clutch of academic qualifications
later, he never thought of himself as anything but a Marlburian,
complete with school-tie worn into maturity. If one school possessed
greater status than the other, it was tempting to assume possession
by association of the one with higher social standing.

Whatever the mode of private evacuation, whether as part of a
school migration or as a solitary child sent by parents to a friend
in the country, it was impressively sizeable, if a bit amorphous.
Richard Titmuss describes it:

> ... the total movement of population during the period of
> transition from peace to war, concluded that about 2,000,000
> individuals left London and other large cities without help
> from the Government ... a study of food registration figures
> and other data suggests, however, that the scale of private
> evacuation diminished as the war went on, at least as markedly
> as did the volume of official evacuation, and possibly in greater
> measure.

In the autumn of 1940 the reaction of the middle-classes to the
savagery of the war was diverse, of course, but often characterized
by bravado. The 'gilded youth' brightened London, then as they
do today, stunning less charismatic citizens with their style, dash
and careless abandon. They made a concerted, if desperate, attempt
to thumb their collective noses at the dangers all too evident in the
skies by gleefully retreating to subterranean West End nightclubs
to fox-trot and jive.

There is no doubt that the blackout and the bombs did provide
a counterpoint of exquisite excitement to the already highly adrena-
lized lives of the young. Just as some children loved playing in the
rubble, rich young things in their twenties found an enhancement
of hedonistic pleasure provided by the presence of so much real
danger. For debonair young men in the forces, who felt every
moment could be their last, the distant sound of sirens wailing, as
they danced cheek-to-cheek with WRNS and WAAFS in Soho
basement bistros, could only titillate.

Piers Paul Read described the lovemaking of Bertrand, a Free
French officer, and his aristocratic, young English girlfriend, Jenny,
in his novel, *The Free Frenchman*. They found joy in a Mayfair flat,

making love to the accompaniment of the sinister thuddings and dronings of bombs crashing outside, with 'the rhythm of their bodies unaffected by the sounds of explosions as if the sheets were a shelter and ecstasy itself a magic protection'. London must have been full of Bertrands and Jennies in 1940, for whom the Blitz became an added aphrodisiac.

Middle-aged and elderly members of the comfortable classes, however, found nothing amusing about any of it, though they struggled to keep stiff upper lips. They certainly disapproved of some of the exaggerated attempts on the part of the 'Sloanes' of the day to emphasize their own larky indifference to danger and the depradations of the war.

Some of the most overcrowded and insanitary shelters, such as the Tilbury archway in East London (where prostitutes continued to solicit and hawkers sold their scrappy goods, while distracted mothers tried to keep their children from soiling the pavements beneath them – in the early days of the Blitz, the government did not provide toilet facilities in the tubes and shelters) became objects of tasteless voyeurism for West End 'tourists'. Constantine Fitzgibbon records:

> Strange as it may seem, some people from the West End used to go sight-seeing to this and other such shelters, even as before the war they would make up jolly parties to visit Chinatown or do a riverside pub-crawl in Wapping. Needless to say, slumming of this sort was not at all popular with the shelterers singing their songs of solidarity in Stepney, and at least one party of sight-seers was quite roughly handled before being ejected.

The vivid sketches Henry Moore drew of families sleeping on murky, draughty, London tube platforms remain fixed in our collective memory of the war. But, as the 1940 figures published by London Transport prove, even during the worst of the Blitz, only about 40 per cent of the city's population used the tubes or open shelters under the archways; most Londoners opted to shelter privately in their garden Andersons or indoors within their Morrisons. With hindsight, we now know that only the deepest tubes were safe shelters, and that shallow underground stations could prove a worse shelter than none at all. On 14 October 1940, for example, 600 people took refuge in Balham tube station. But, since the tube was only some thirty feet beneath Balham High Road, when the station was bombed, burst underground water and gas mains added to the torment of the luckless Londoners caught within. Virtually every succeeding month saw some shallow city tube and those harbouring within it meet with disaster: St Pancras (forty-seven feet below ground level); Holloway (forty-five feet); Bounds Green (thirty-two feet) all sustained direct hits. Moorgate was burnt out on 29 December and a bomb blast at Bank, on 11 January 1941, caused the road to collapse overhead, killing 111.

The government dithered as to what to do about the people and their 'self-chosen' shelters. At first, it cautioned them to abandon the communal shelters and stay at home. Later, when it became obvious that people could not be dissuaded from seeking protection in the tubes, the government attempted to make tube shelters cleaner, better ventilated, and fitted out with improved sanitary facilities. Amazingly, the health of the people did not seem adversely affected by the overcrowding and dirt of the tubes. Minor irritants – scabies and lice – did increase, but an anticipated upsurge of serious diseases, such as tuberculosis or bronchitis, simply did not materialize. Open displays of hysteria or neurosis, shouting or panic, were remarkably absent, too. As Fitzgibbon reports:

> There was no increase in insanity: there was less suicides: drunkenness declined by over 50 per cent: there was less disorderly behaviour in public: and only juvenile delinquency increased, which increase can be largely attributed to the break-up of family life.

But, in spite of such sterling behaviour in the face of depressing circumstances, the middle- and upper-classes avoided using the public shelters. Aesthetically, they were unappealing places: endless seas of grimy faces shone in the murk, like figures from Dante doomed to hell. Perhaps more concrete fears of infestation or of catching a contagious disease put them off. Whatever the reason, such shelters were hardly ever used by the privileged classes. Fitzgibbon argues that the middle-classes felt a strong psychological antipathy towards displaying any fear of death, reckoning it 'not quite cricket' to do so. Perhaps he's right, but even had they wanted, in his words, to 'go down and down into the deepest of tubes', they didn't – certain that such an action would have betrayed that most craven of emotions, cowardice. Thus they toughed it out above ground. Or they took flight discreetly.

Fleeing, too, had to be done circumspectly, and at one's own expense, if it was not to seem somewhat 'infra-dig', went the thinking of the better-off. Any government-sponsored arrangements smacked of weedily succumbing to the power of the State instead of relying on individual resourcefulness. (Think of the way many of the genteel classes today would rather dig into their meagre savings to pay for a Harley Street consultation than queue in a public hospital waiting-room for similar treatment – often by the same consultant – on the NHS.)

'I was evacuated by my mother but I don't think you could call me an evacuee,' Brenda Bancroft said, in genuine astonishment, when I asked her for an interview last year. A pretty, former actress in her early fifties, whom I have known for over twenty years, she had never told me of her evacuation experience, even though our children had been school playmates in the sixties and we have spent many hours together. An intrepid single parent, who has steered her three lively daughters and two sons through the best schools and universities of the land by dint of saving and hard work as a market researcher, it was clear she had no vision of herself as an evacuee. 'I never had a tag around my neck or brown lunch box and got taken to the railway station by my school,' she explained, 'so I never considered myself an evacuee, but I suppose I must be, of course.'

Brenda Bancroft's confusion as to her wartime status is mirrored by many of her class. Although she was indeed sent away – in her case from Southampton to Pangbourne, Oxfordshire – because she had none of the accoutrements of the child evacuee, which now symbolize that experience, she couldn't imagine herself as having been one. Her perceptions were shared by many others of the better-off evacuees I contacted. If they had been evacuated with an entire school, they deemed the epithet even less apposite to them, I discovered, as if inclusion in a merry, privileged group had removed them completely from the lot of the common herd. The image of an inner-city child travelling with little else but a grubby chocolate bar and an orange seems to have lodged itself permanently in the public imagination. But the term 'evacuee' can, of course, be widened to encompass any child shifted from natural parents in one area to foster-parents in another; or in the case of schools, from one site to another.

Brenda Bancroft, aged eight in 1940, recalls her hasty departure from her mother, a horse-racing buff, who seemed a bit scatty in her manner of kitting Brenda out for the trip to Oxfordshire. Brenda remembers she was inadequately dressed for the chilly autumn day, and took little with her but a scarred brown suitcase and the skirt and sweater she wore to catch the train:

> I went to the most gorgeous house in the Oxfordshire hills and joined a lovely mother and her two daughters. The mother knew my mother remotely, I suppose, though I think the foster home had been arranged by my school. I just know that I never looked back and never felt homesick. I could tell that my foster-mother was appalled at my threadbare wardrobe, but she was too polite to say anything. I'm sure I'd been sort of dragged up because I remember being stunned by everyone's beautiful manners. I'm positive that I learned everything I know about how to behave and how to relate to other people from this family. I was an only child . . . a poor little rich girl, I guess.

Brenda's story is significant, I think, because it emphasizes one very important point about the middle-class evacuation. As these children didn't have to cope, as poorer children had to, with the cultural differences and feelings of being an outsider – of sometimes being looked down upon – their emotional baggage was much lighter. They often had less to learn about day to day adaptation to different social customs, or how to respond to verbal cues which seemed totally foreign. Many of them recalled having to deal with unfamiliar *qualities* of life; but not having to deal with perplexing, concrete differences in morals and manners permitted them to be more open to shadings of experience in their new environments. Brenda was able to note the harmonious relationships and good manners, arising out of natural kindness, in the family she found herself entering. In a subtle, abstract way, the good fortune of being middle-class in the first place often appeared to be reinforced by encountering experiences which enriched rather than dismayed or frightened the evacuee child.

Hilary Granger, fifty-nine, a retired Hertfordshire English teacher, now living in Woodbridge, Suffolk, and the happily married mother of a grown son and daughter, sums up her evacuation experience succinctly: 'There were a few physical hardships but no emotional ones.' Like Brenda, she was an only child. She blesses having been evacuated from a lonely existence at a day school in Nottingham to the ordered and happy, communal life at a boarding school in Leicestershire, only twenty miles from Nottingham in distance, but light years away in atmosphere. There she found the extended family she had longed for as a shy, rather literary, ten year old in the city. Her school, Hollygirt, was evacuated on 1 September 1939, to Billesdon manor. They travelled by Trent motor-coaches, she recalls precisely, to this handsome residence, nestling in the hunting and farming countryside between Leicester and Uppingham.

It had been let to the school for the duration of the war by a kindly, bachelor colonel, who also handed over all his fine Hepplewhite furniture, oil paintings and gramophone records. Japonica and wisteria hung from the stone frontage and fires glowed in the fireplaces. The manor was the acme of civilization but, despite the fireplaces, as deeply, bone-chillingly cold as only English country manor houses can be. Hilary remembers she:

. . . reacted to the shock news that I was leaving home with tears and excitement, as anyone would who has been given no prior warning. I remember someone pointing to a stark newspaper poster, proclaiming 'Germany invades Poland', as we drove through the city. We, by no means, resembled the woebegone prototype of the wartime evacuees, sent miles by train to sit long hours in village halls waiting to be selected by reluctant residents with whom they were to be billeted. We travelled comfortably, chatting excitedly about Billesdon and what we would find at the manor.

I was very unhappy at first because I'd never been away before. I had many tearful nights. It was bitterly cold – an Elizabethan house. I slept in the old children's nursery, which was furnished with Edwardian wallpaper and dado on the cornices. We were over the kitchen and this was the only heating we had. I suffered acutely from chilblains even though we wore socks in bed. A friend of mine had chilblains all up the backs of her legs. We had nothing to keep us warm but a hot water bottle each and the rising heat from the kitchen. Three years later, I was entrusted with an electric fire when I moved to the top of the house.

Many of us were 'only' children and this experience of having to adapt to life with others was certainly very valuable to us. It was a unifying experience.

But the school routine was rather boring. Bells were forbidden during the war and we were roused in the morning by the

sound of gongs. If it was your turn for early morning piano
practice, you had to speed quickly down to the lounge to pound
away at your scales. In the winter, the great log fire would be
smoking away without making any appreciable impact on the
temperature. Then followed, relentlessly – breakfast, bed-
making, prayers, lessons, lunch, washing-up duties, games,
letters home, tea, prep, supper, bed. There were also the little
duties which we organized ourselves on a rota system. 'Doing
the blackout' was one. All windows had to be completely
shielded during the war, and if so much as a chink of light was
seen from the outside the local warden would hot-foot around
with his reprimand. Another duty was the filling of hot water
bottles – those hot water bottles were a great comfort!

In the evenings, we would toast our bread over the open fire
– we usually had bread and marg or bread and dripping for
supper. And we could listen to the radio, either the 'Schools
Radio' or 'Current Affairs'. We were aware of the progress of
the war. None of us had any fears about defeat. We could not
really believe that anything dreadful would happen to us,
although we did have to go down to the cellars when Coventry,
and the Midlands generally, was being bombed. I also heard a
stray V-1 exploding in a field nearby in November 1944.

I liked the good family atmosphere at Billesdon. It was
salutary for a protected, introspective child like me. But it was
monotonous. There was little for youngsters at boarding school
to do during the war.

The shock encountered by many middle-class children sent to
'safe' boarding schools was, as Hilary Granger points out, the shock
of physical discomfort. British boarding schools were, ironically,
still heavily influenced by the teachings of the German 'health and
beauty' martinet, Dr Daniel Gottlieb Moritz Schreber (1842–1911).
He was fanatical about children's posture and regular sleeping
habits. Too much warmth smacked of sensuality to him and hence
hard, iron mattresses, minimal blankets, cold water and brisk runs
in the frosty dawn before breakfast, callisthenics, and outdoor sports
in all weathers were his cherished recipes for growing children.

Food, too, could be spartan at these beautifully appointed schools,
a condition of life naturally exacerbated by wartime rationing.
Hilary Granger recently found the diary she had kept at Billesdon
throughout the war, and opened it with keen anticipation. She had

been a bookish child, fond of Jane Austen and the Brontës, and was rather hoping to find some early philosophical ruminations. Instead, what she discovered was entry upon entry about 'food, beautiful food'. The outbreak of war provoked Hilary to write:

> September 3rd. We went to the eleven o'clock service at Church. Towards the end of the service the vicar told us that war had been declared. We had sausages for dinner and damsons and custard . . .

And in the days that followed, she stuck to her central theme:

> September 4th. Peeled apples and went to the village for some washing soda. Cold meat and fruit for dinner . . .

> September 5th. Peeled pears in the morning and played. Had a letter from Mummy. I had cold meat, potatoes and salad, jelly and custard.
>
> After dinner I wrote to Auntie Mollie and went for a walk across the fields.

While meals were plain fare, and luxuries such as butter and eggs were strictly rationed ('one egg every two weeks and butter on Sundays'), Hilary's diet was clearly very nutritious, full of fresh fruit, protein, and a balanced and unexcessive amount of carbohydrate. How different from the usual diet of the poor with its reliance on bread and dripping, or bread and chips. It is interesting to note that the more privileged had bread and dripping once a day, if at all – it was Hilary Granger's boarding school's supper meal only – and it was regarded as a mid-meal snack, not as a basic.

One passion both middle-class and poorer-class evacuee could share, when transferred from city to country, was a new-found delight in the countryside – if not always for the fruit and vegetables it bore, then at least for the beauty of its fields and trees. Robin Mitchell, a Sloane Square deputy bank manager, now fifty-six, who was evacuated with St Paul's School in London to the countryside in Berks., found the transfer magical:

> I was at St Paul's Junior School when the war broke out, the only child of a banking father. We lived in Hounslow and father was an air raid warden. One night hundreds of incendiaries came down and it seemed a marvel to me. The worst night – worst for father . . . I thought it was great – there were

all these unexploded bombs sticking out of the pavements in cones – they were duds. For a boy, it was huge fun – I'd be panic-stricken now.

It was at about this time that my school was transferred – all 153 of us – to Crowthorne in Berkshire and I think it was during the time of the worst of the 1940 blitzes.* I know it wasn't long after I'd seen that miraculous street of dud incendiaries in my neighbourhood.

We were divided into school parties and I cycled with about forty boys the thirty-five miles to Crowthorne. I know it seems incredible that we should have travelled that far on our bikes but cycling was different those days. Being wartime, there was little traffic on the roads and no nasty people around to make it a danger. Our goods had been sent ahead by train so we weren't particularly heavily laden.

The major part of the school was in a beautiful mansion with hostels in the village for any overspill of teachers or boys. We all had jobs to help run our separate hostels, I was called a 'Fuel' – there were four or five of us – and this meant collecting firewood in the grounds for the stoking up of the fires. There would be fifteen to twenty boys lodging in each hostel. We had a likeable widow in charge of ours. Though our actual rulers were the prefects – about four of them. I remember they were not very interested in our problems about collecting kindling and logs, but just wanted to see we had the fires going. I always had a terrible time getting the fires to start.

Whatever the weather, we cycled and we were all very fit. I was only there for a year but I remember it was a great adventure. I take sentimental journeys back there each year and I try not to examine the main building too carefully. It's a bit tatty now – a teacher training college or something. I love driving up that long path and seeing the squirrels and the trees. When I drive up it, I visualize all the cycle racks which used to be alongside the driveway when we were there. I get in

*I was amused to see that Robin Mitchell, a meticulous banker, is just as confused about his actual date of evacuation as are all of the middle-aged evacuees I've interviewed. Unless they kept diaries, as Hilary Granger did, few could pinpoint the exact date. Children's minds tend to focus on events such as their own birthdays, but others are opaque. I am only able to remember the date of my own evacuation from the Far East with my mother in November 1940, because my diplomat father's staff, Chinese predominantly, wrote us a farewell note on 6 November and gave us a present of two garish yellow vases – proverbial 'white elephant' gifts for a couple of frightened evacuees told to travel light and fast.

touch with my boyhood. My wife and three grown daughters think it a bit odd, I suspect. But I'm a bit of a lone wolf and I like my annual return. It calms me down. I can't explain why – maybe it's because I remember those days as a time of innocence.

For many boys attending posh city schools with rigid routines, the country break the town bombings necessitated, meant a welcome change from overly structured and sophisticated lives. Robin Mitchell's wood-gathering in icy weather under the supervision of prefects seems nothing short of Dickensian, but it remains a happy memory to him, largely because it allowed him freedom, and time to himself. His sentiments were shared by others.

Anthony Sampson, journalist and historian, told a *Daily News* reporter in an interview (30 June 1987) about his Westminster days in wartime:

> I was part of the Westminster generation, forty-five years ago, which was never at Westminster. In wartime the most urban of all schools became the most rural, scattered between houses in Hertfordshire, and I bicycled twelve miles a day between them. The school's dispersal may have been the best thing that could have happened. It released its pupils from stiff collars and white ties and propelled them into corduroy shorts and open necks. It turned little toffs into country bumpkins. To my relief, instead of sports we dug the garden or picked cherries.

For the poor child, evacuation to the country was often confusing and hurtful, with strangers inviting him or her to abandon cherished habits; for the middle-class evacuee, it could liberate. Eva Figes remembered her evacuation year at Cirencester, when she was about twelve, as a time of learning to ride a bicycle ('Life was like riding a bike, riding a bike was life. Exhilarating.'), and luxuriating in unaccustomed freedom. Eva, a refugee from Germany, felt at home in the England she came to, aged ten. Only in hindsight did she reflect that it must have been miserable for her mother, lonely in London, and struggling to maintain her dressmaking skills against the impossible odds presented by the rationing of fabric.

> It must have been a hard year for her, quite alone in that small flat, husband and children away, the strain of heavy bombing at nights. But for me it was easy, and I was too young to have developed a sense of guilt at my own disloyalty. I was happy

away from home. I revelled in my new-found sense of independence, finding things out, being a person, riding a bike as though I had grown wings. I was not homesick. If I was happy to see my parents, the promise of a good square meal had as much to do with it as hugs and kisses.

Perhaps it was because, even as a very small child, I had been conscious of a secret solitary nucleus inside which nobody could reach. It held pain, but also dreams, and I needed to be withdrawn to allow it to grow. The separateness of being away at school gave it time to grow, to find roots in friendly soil, sprout branches and blossom into the first spring of creative imagination, leaf into rapturous life, roots fed with constant thirst for knowledge. It was only later, after the brief interlude of time and place was over, that the strains of war and its effect on my family began to impinge on me.

Eva Figes, like Hilary Granger, recalled that physical discomforts were acute, however much the joys of self-discovery served to mute them. While she exulted in the lack of regimentation in her small village school, she did not like the constant gnawing hunger felt both at school and at her foster-home, nor the cold and damp in her basement lavatory where the air whistled through cracks, chilling her as she washed and dressed.

But a certain spunkiness buoyed up even the most privileged of children, and many of them managed to ignore the physical hardships and embrace the challenges, especially intellectual ones, which confronted them. Beatrice Musgrave, an editor and writer, who is now embarking, in her early sixties, on a new career as a London psychotherapist, is convinced that what she learnt from evacuation turned her into the 'achiever' she became in college and after. Beatrice, like Eva Figes, was a refugee from Germany; she arrived in London in 1938. She had already been to boarding school in Switzerland and so separations from her indulgent parents were not new. The company of her younger sister eased the first brief, and checkered, evacuation experience undertaken with her private day school. They were sent to Reading in September 1939:

This really was evacuation, totally different from the earlier experience of arriving in London from Germany and enjoying a quite glamorous time with our banking relatives, who'd already settled in England, and treated us to teas in lovely hotels. My sister and I were billeted with three different families outside Reading, all of quite different backgrounds, two very hostile to having young girls dumped on them. One, an old clergyman and his wife, more or less forbade us to be in the house during the day. Another, a vicious father with a terrified daughter, accused us of scribbling graffiti on his lavatory walls and got rid of us that way. The third family – a post office sorter with wife and son – were kind and cosy and provided our first experience of simple, grass-roots English life.

Then, in 1940, we moved – as a family – to Yorkshire to escape the bombs. My father established his business there and we were sent to Bradford Grammar School – a marvellous, formative period. We had family in Bradford who had come there in the late 1800s, but in the local village outside Bradford, people weren't quite sure at first whether we were in the same category as some Channel Island evacuees who had come there. They liked us and we had a great many school friends, but my parents were never accepted into local circles.

Though my education had been disrupted several times by then, I did well and adapted. Being good with language and literature was a great help. I didn't miss my German roots as I had them with me, and blending them with English life was enriching. Of course, English ways were different but how do you quantify? At thirteen one learns so quickly! Language difficulties lasted only about a week. I came top in English and seemed set fair for Oxford entry. I think my chequered experience – refugee, evacuee – was a spur to achievement – the need to be successful, to get to Oxford, to have a career, may all have had something to do with early disruption and having to make one's way in a new country.

Of course, the onset of war had alarmed us – it alarmed everybody, didn't it? My mother and father had never told us about Hitler's intentions – we were very protected by our parents – and so I took it in much the same spirit as my schoolmates – somewhat off-handedly, I think.

Few middle-class evacuees seemed to have had a clear idea as to what the war was about, or exactly why they were shunted off to the country. Conversely, Susan Isaacs reported in her *Cambridge Evacuation Survey* that quite a number of working-class children were deeply disturbed by fears of their parents dying beneath the bombs in the cities, and wanted to return home as a result. Separation anxieties, combined with fears associated with the war, prevented them from settling in to their new billets. Worry about their parents did not appear to afflict many well-heeled children in their boarding school bolt-holes or comfortable country lodgings. Eva Figes, among others, never gave her mother a thought until much later, when the war ended. Presumably, this is what Eva's mother had intended. Middle-class parents wished to buffer their children against the reality of the war while working-class parents discussed it openly with them (see Chapter 4). It's dubious whether middle-class parents did their offspring any great favour by 'protecting' them in this way.

As a bright young student, Hilary Granger tried to penetrate the silence surrounding war as her school diary records. She listened to current affairs programmes, and possessed a fascination for war news fed by her school vicar. She says she has her grandmother to thank for the curiosity she had about the war, since her mother sought to shield her from life's unpleasantness. Her grandmother, a strong-minded, left-wing feminist and friend of Vera Brittain's, had made a point of taking Hilary to an air-raid shelter in the centre of Nottingham when she was nine. In her grandmother's canon, it was wrong to mollycoddle children. In any event, her efforts to prepare Hilary for the war had not been sufficient, for she says she felt 'catapulted' into the process of evacuation, feeling there was something catastrophic in the air but not quite knowing what. Her grandmother had fought a losing battle, Hilary admits. In the cocoon-like school she was sent to, war was equated with the teachers receiving more generous ration coupons than their charges and hence larger portions of butter; and originally elegant school uniforms (kilts by the famous Edinburgh outfitters, Romanes & Patterson) became frayed in time and had to be replaced by simpler, machine-made garments.

Some former evacuees, such as the theatre director and polymath, Jonathan Miller,* assert the buffering surrounding them was so total that it became more than a cloud of unknowing, rather a palpable fog, shutting out reality altogether. He remembers that when he was seven, his psychiatrist father and the rest of the family moved around England with gypsy-like regularity, not staying anywhere for more than six months. He swears he attended at least eight schools between Dunkirk and D-Day, and remembers living

*See Chapter 9, p. 153.

the life of a nomad for four years. Further mystification was in store for him, as he explained in *The Evacuees*:

> I was not suddenly taken away from my parents and I did not have to live through the horror of bed-wetting in strange houses. Nothing like that. But I *was* evacuated. I was moved out of London, away from a settled home; and for reasons which I was too young to understand travelled here and there in the depths of rural England without staying long enough in any one place to feel that I ever put down roots . . .
>
> And then my father seemed to vanish. Not with any painful suddenness. But here, there and everywhere, he casually disappeared and the smell of turps and housepaint appeared in his place. And then he reappeared in uniform, mysteriously renovated by his absence, spruced up in a new coat of khaki trimmed with a Sam Browne belt.

His father, it transpired, had gone off to Aldershot for basic army medical corps training in 1939, and had anxiously urged his wife to find a safe haven for the family somewhere in the West Country. Both he and his wife were panicked by the thought of a German invasion, but said nothing to their small son. His sense of dread grew, however, the more he was kept in the dark:

> We were staying, I think, near Monmouth, right on the Wye, a short distance from Tintern; and the only thing which does come back from that hot dark summer is a sense of drugged rural heat, hay, and the hallucinatory memory of my father, heroically uniformed, standing among the harvest sheaves, taking a glass of cider with the local farmer. I don't think I can remember a single specific reference to the war. Or at least not as such. But there must have been something which got through to me, since the memory of that delicious corn-coloured heat is poisoned with suggestions of danger too. Perhaps it's something which I read into it backwards, now, after everything I've heard about the period as an adult. But I don't think so. The sweating stillness of that Wye valley, almost thirty years ago, still frightens me much more than it pleases. There *was* an air of dreadful pregnancy and I can still hear the cool unhurried morse of a cuckoo hidden in those distant woods spelling out the orders for some horrible but as yet unrealised enactment.

It has also been remarked that the war engendered a certain seriousness in the rather owlish, well-behaved, middle-class children who lived through it. In a profile of the writer, Kingsley Amis, called 'The Entertainer in Old Age' by Bryan Appleyard, published in *The Times* (4 September 1986), the journalist suggested that the wartime evacuation of City of London School to Marlborough had a profound effect on the adolescent Amis, and bred in him a near vocational fervour for the pursuit of literature. Discussing Amis's friendship at St John's College, Oxford, with the poet, Philip Larkin, Appleyard states the novelist and poet 'shared a reticence' about their reverence for literature, and gives two 'obvious' reasons for it: 'First the war – most knew they would have to fight, and this engendered a certain seriousness about work. Second, there was an antipathy to the grand self-consciousness of modernism.'

These evacuees – their expensively paid-for safety in luxurious surroundings notwithstanding – knew little of the normal fripperies of the youth culture so familiar to us today. Hilary Granger explains:

> I think you could say we missed out on gaiety, on wearing bright clothes which set us apart as a group, as teenagers do today. We went straight from shabby wartime wardrobes to post-war Utility. In other words, progressing from a plain adolescence to our matronly twenties. None of us Billesdon Old Girls have divorced, we find at our reunions. And all have tended to work. I've worked for thirty years.

It's possible to conclude that cushioned disruption tended to produce dedication rather than neurosis, but these middle-class children did miss out on something – frivolity, perhaps – joy, certainly. At least they experienced a certain solidity in their lives, grey though it might have been. What, however, of the overseas evacuees? How did they fare thousands, not hundreds, of miles from home?

Evacuation Overseas:
Some Succeeded, Others Not

As the European countries collapsed before the German invaders in the summer of 1940, and England seemed destined to become the next battlefield, many parents became edgy about the effectiveness of sending their children to rural billets and began to consider the possibility of sending them to overseas 'havens' – the Dominions and the United States. As before, a two-tiered evacuation programme emerged: the private and the government-sponsored. The statistics provided for private evacuation overseas are sketchy, but some put the figure as high as 4000 children and 1000 adults.

It is, of course, far easier to establish the numbers involved in the official evacuation organized by CORB, the Children's Overseas Reception Board, a London-based group headed by Geoffrey Shakespeare (later Sir Geoffrey). Some newspapers coined the ghastly pun – 'CORB . . . Limeys' – to describe these evacuees, but happily it did not stick. Under the CORB scheme, some 3500 were shipped abroad: 836 to the US; 1532 to Canada; 576 to Australia; 353 to South Africa and 203 to New Zealand. It was decided officially that the children should go to private homes and attend local schools overseas in order to feel part of the social fabric rather than alien. Kind invitations from homes abroad had poured into the Foreign Office with the declaration of war in 1939 (tender feelings were evoked in overseas hearts at the thought of the danger threatening the youth of the 'Mother Country'); therefore, the Foreign Office knew the children were wanted. However, it allowed its own chauvinism to surface by refusing equally generous offers from Latin American countries anxious to harbour the children. The evacuees were to go to 'English-speaking' countries only was the stiff response accorded South American hospitality.

While the government had dithered about shipping children overseas all through May, events galvanized decision-making in June. On the day – 18 June 1940 – that France capitulated – the War Cabinet, a coalition, endorsed the scheme for overseas' evacuation for children under fifteen. This was not effected without internecine party squabbling: Labour's Clement Attlee, then Lord Privy Seal, implored the House of Commons to establish the machinery for the plan with 'utmost urgency', while the Tory Prime Minister Winston Churchill grumbled his disapproval.* On the 18th of July, Churchill wrote to Sir John Anderson, the Home Secretary:

> I certainly do not propose to send a message by the senior child to Mr Mackenzie King, or by the junior child either. If I sent a message by anyone, it would be that I entirely deprecate any stampede from this country at the present time.

Out of context, Churchill's heavy irony is confusing: he apparently didn't want the presence of the children in foreign countries to be interpreted by anyone, whether the Canadian Prime Minister or Hitler, as a sign that Britain was flagging and defeatism was in the air. Churchill was a firm believer in seeking safety at home, as we have seen in Chapter 3, when he suggested to Lord Ismay that citizens should dig themselves more deeply into their shelters and keep safe by staying put. To rush to safety elsewhere smacked of 'rats-and-sinking-ships' to him. Similar examples of sterling patriotism had rallied the people to his side in the previous months of the Blitz, but with 6 June and the rout at Dunkirk fresh in their minds, coupled with the defeat of France, parents and officials chose to ignore the old bulldog.

Added to the fears of encroaching German invaders were some confused beliefs, fanned by the popular press, that it was downright unpatriotic to stay in London at all if you were not actively involved in the war effort. In a front page article in the *Daily Express*, Lord Beaverbrook urged the citizenry (through a staff correspondent's pen) to get out of London. The 11 July article exhorted: 'If there is no important reason why you should stay in the area, move out . . . It is important that areas should be as clear as possible in case of military action . . .'

Today, people who were overseas evacuees usually apologize for the actions of their parents in sending them overseas, feeling it

---

*Not all historians of the period believe there was internecine squabbling between Attlee and Churchill over overseas evacuation, but rather that Attlee craftily managed to get the legislation passed because Churchill was 'nodding'.

was a faintly unpatriotic and privileged way out of the mêlée. Investigation of the movement, however, reveals one crucial point: it was not a class-biased exodus confined to the well-to-do. Sir Geoffrey Shakespeare had made it plain from the start that he wanted a fair 'class mix' and this was indeed what he achieved. The government bore the brunt of the expense, paying the children's sea-going fares in the majority of cases.

What customarily dictated whether or not a parent sent a child overseas was the presence of a family member in the host country abroad, or that the parent already knew something, at least, about the country where the child was bound. This was particularly true in the case of parents sending their children to Australia and New Zealand; some had heard of antipodean spots from relatives which left them with cherished thoughts of sun, sea and a gloriously free outback. The idea that their children were going to safety and also to radiantly healthy outdoor places often compensated in parents' minds for the misery of placing so many thousands of miles between them and their offspring.

What concerned some parliamentarians about the overseas evacuees was the thought that these small emigres might become 'forgotten children'; over a prolonged period of time their absence might consign them to a kind of far-flung *oubliette*. No one need have worried for the parents left behind kept their children's images fresh in their minds by writing to them constantly and sending radio messages via the BBC's 'Children's Hour', created before the war but ideal for beaming just such contact overseas. If there was any 'forgetting' done, it was on the part of the children who, if they didn't actually forget their parents, adjusted so readily to their new land that they felt like foreigners on return to Britain in 1945. Quite a few of the CORB evacuees were unable to re-adjust on returning to their native land, and eventually emigrated for good after the war. This was especially true of those evacuees who were in their early teens when they embarked on the voyage to North America, and were subsequently absorbed into the seductive high-school culture they found in Toronto, Des Moines or Boston.*

---

*One of the youngsters interviewed by *New York Times* feature writer, Elizabeth Ogg, in an article written in its 11 November 1946 supplement about the post-war lives of evacuees, quoted the comment about American boys by seventeen-year-old Laura Wales (who had lived for three years, from thirteen to sixteen, in Ohio): ' "They're more exciting. I'd much prefer an American husband to an English one." We never found out if she did, in fact, marry an American, but it is not unlikely.' Girls, especially, fell for the 'American-pie', high-school fizz and pazazz, 'bobby-sox and crooner' backdrop to their daily lives and decided to stay.

The distance involved in these evacuations also raised the vexed question of guardianship. Wouldn't the foster-parents in the US and Canada, and the other Dominions, need special powers over their charges, particularly where medical matters were concerned (the 'go-ahead' required to authorize emergency operations or blood transfusions, for example)? In particular, what would happen if an adolescent evacuee went wild in the freer North American atmosphere? If discipline appeared necessary would the natural parents in Britain be able to dictate from afar what form it took, or would the overseas foster-parents be expected to take the teenager in hand? Conversely, what if the adoptive parents were over-strict? These prickly matters were resolved by a new law.

After much debate, it was decided to appoint Britain's top representative in the US and the Dominions (the British Ambassador in the US; the Governors-General in the Dominions) to act as 'sole guardian' in accordance with the laws of England 'notwithstanding that the child may not be . . . domiciled (in England)'. The Temporary Migration (Guardianship) Act was passed on 12 June 1941 and, as American historian, Carlton Jackson points out, bestowed many a headache on the British diplomats responsible for its enactment abroad, bequeathing as it did the responsibility of 'repatriating the children after the war if the parents could not', a guarantee built into the Act. (A small number of British parents were indeed delinquent in their payments.)

Parents were asked to pay six shillings a week per child into an overseas fund; the monies were put into escrow by CORB. (Parents of children evacuated within Britain, who had to pay more than the six shillings a week per child required for overseas evacuees,* were bitterly resentful.) Later, as the war dragged on and some of the CORB children were still with North American hosts after four years, there were complaints from the foster-parents about the inadequate funding; but most North American foster-parents were generous about supporting their additional financial burden even though it frequently entailed hardship for them. Marion Dunham, a Boston member of the English-Speaking Union, commented in 1943 that: 'Many American sponsors are finding it financially very hard to carry on for four years when they imagined it would be for one.'

Fluctuations in sympathy for the evacuees differed, intriguingly,

*See Chapter 2, pp. 22–3.

between British and foreign foster-parents. In 1939, rural British foster-parents were sometimes testy about having to care for children who were not in any apparent danger during the time of the Phoney War; their impatience tended to evaporate as soon as the bombs dropped in earnest during the autumn of 1940 and the spring of 1941 at the height of the Blitz, and even at the time of the Third Evacuation in 1944–5 when the V-1 and V-2 rockets were sent flying over southeast England. For the overseas families, patriotism and protective fervour were at their peak during the early stages of the war, especially until December 1941 when America was still neutral. But American foster-parents became increasingly luke-warm towards their charges after the US entered the war and they were faced with their own privations.

A small number of host families in the US, in particular, felt they were being exploited by British parents because of the inadequate funds sent to them. When they were not feeling bitter about money, they were wondering *when* their young charges were going to go home. Their feelings swung from one extreme to another (perhaps logical extremes owing to the long tenure of surrogate parenthood they were enduring) and some tried legally to adopt their British children. The foster-parents' painful and conflicting feelings were not helped, I suspect, by their lack of proper custodial powers over the children denied by the 1941 Guardianship Act. Their rights remained shadowy throughout the war, whereas British foster-parents knew where they stood, a fact that made their position much more bearable for them. As we know, once they had passed muster in the eyes of the local area billeting officer, they were automatically accorded *in loco parentis* status. (See footnote concerning their exact legal position on p. 81).

Relations between Britain and America were at an all-time high in 1940; the 'special relationship' was very special, indeed. Some historians say that American generosity – whether it took the form of housewives knitting socks for the 'Bundles for Britain' campaign (two million knitted garments were sent to the UK from one American relief agency alone) or the Lend-Lease equipment and services provided by the government itself – sprang from guilt feelings. 'Poor little England is taking it on the chin while we sit here in the land of plenty' spoke the voice of American conscience. Whatever the reason for this great outpouring of emotion and generosity – whether from guilt or goodness – it was quantifiable. Food supplies from the US to Britain acted as a lifeline at the time:

800 million pounds of meat and fish products; a thousand million pounds of grain; 800 million pounds of fruit and vegetables; and 800 million pounds of milk and egg products (those famous dried eggs!) were shipped across the Atlantic.

Before the children could set foot on board ship, the British government had to decide on *whose* ship. President Roosevelt expressed himself willing to have them ferried across the Atlantic in American ships, especially after Germany had promised 'safe conduct'. However, Churchill felt compromised by this accord, wondering what the Germans would expect from neutral America in return (Britain needed America's Lend-Lease supplies and didn't want them jeopardized). So CORB turned to Dutch and Polish ships to transport the children. Though Holland had been overrun by the Germans in May 1940, most of its fleet had escaped to England (this is why the *Volendam* was used to transport evacuee children on 28 August 1940, for example).

British parents were unaware of the behind-the-scenes diplomatic disputes between nations over 'safe conduct', and signed their children up for evacuation in good faith. For those neither clinging nor over-protective parents who had decided that overseas evacuation was preferable to the home-based variety in the first place (particularly if they possessed a more cosmopolitan outlook than some of the more provincial parents for whom a 35-mile separation could seem vast), the intricacies of the voyage did not weigh on their minds overmuch – not, at least, until the evacuee ships began to be torpedoed. Before this, their fears, when they had any, centred round issues such as whether the children would lose their accents and general British stamp, and whether on their return they would be competent to sit the difficult (by comparison to high schools in America then) British college and university entrance examinations.

One of the many documents parents were required to sign was one which completely exonerated the government should the child suffer death or injury either en route or in residence abroad. There was no cavilling about this from parents in the summer of 1940, although when the *City of Benares* was sunk by a German U-boat on 17 September 1940, killing 256 people – seventy-seven of them children* – they might have wondered why they had not been more far-sighted.

*These statistics on the *Benares* fatalities were kindly given to me by the meticulous journalist, Ralph Barker. See Sources, p. 170 for details of his definitive book on the disaster.

Two parents who remained adamant about not evacuating their children overseas were King George VI and Queen Elizabeth, who refused to send the two princesses, Elizabeth and Margaret Rose, then thirteen and eight respectively, to Canada as they had been urged to do by many advisors. The Royal children *were* evacuated – but no further than Windsor Castle for most of the year, punctuated by intermittent stays with their mother in Scotland for holidays. They were tutored privately, but otherwise led normal lives, joining the Brownies and Girl Guides and 'Digging for Victory'. On 14 October 1940, Princess Elizabeth spoke to the overseas evacuees on 'Children's Hour', wishing them good luck and thanking their overseas hosts. The Royal Family did not escape the direct effects of the war. In September 1940, Buckingham Palace was hit by a bomb and the chapel was destroyed, causing the Queen [now the Queen Mother] to make her famous comment: 'I'm glad we've been bombed. It makes me feel I can look the East End in the face.' The public loved it.

But while Britain was relieved to be able to keep its princesses at home – newspaper pictures of their untroubled faces and trim, tailored figures going about their girlish duties were especially solacing during the Blitz – no one felt like casting stones at the parents of overseas evacuees. At the time everyone thought it was their business and theirs alone. Perhaps such universal tolerance has a simple explanation: parents of overseas evacuees were in a minority – even with the less precise figures known about private evacuation, the total number of children and mothers, or children alone, did not exceed 20,000. When this figure is contrasted with the First Evacuation, which affected hundreds of thousands of women and children, the overseas movement can be put in its true perspective. Because it was more dramatic initially and given so much overseas publicity, this evacuation has tended to remain more vivid in Britain's national memory than the others: North American newspapers recorded each 'cute' remark or observation an evacuee came out with. On 1 October 1940, in a front-page story, the *New York Times* excitedly reported – 'They don't like boiled eggs in cups!'

During the war people were not considered 'unpatriotic' for opting to send their children abroad, even though their children today sometimes *do* feel guilty for having gone. Before the sinking of the *City of Benares*, when overseas evacuation acquired its own edge of terror, this option seemed perfectly sensible. Dame Josephine

Barnes, the distinguished obstetrician (twenty-seven years old at
the start of the war), delivered hundreds of babies in straitened
wartime conditions both in London and Oxford. She assured me
that:

> Many of us gave serious consideration to sending our children
> abroad. We just had no idea at all in the spring and early
> summer of 1940 what might strike us . . . It could have been
> anything – poison gas, German occupation, whatever – we
> didn't know. I didn't have my first child, Penelope, until 1943.
> She was an infant during the flying bombs episode, and of
> course too young for evacuation abroad then. But I certainly
> would have considered it seriously had she been born earlier.
> I kept saying to myself when she did arrive, 'I don't want this
> baby to die.' I used to take great comfort in the knowledge that
> I had American cousins in Bronxville, New York, who would
> have any child of mine with them if I'd asked. The idea of
> being critical of any parent who sent their children overseas
> never entered my mind.

There is evidence that, although parents thought they were doing
the right thing by sending their children away, it was agonizing for
them to do so. That tireless journal writer, Vera Brittain, with
her observant eye, allied to an ability to convey deeper, personal
emotions, wrote of putting daughter Shirley, nine, and son John,
twelve, on an ocean steamer bound for North America. Shirley, née
Catlin, later Williams, and her brother, who later called himself
Brittain-Catlin, were rather carefree about the whole business, as
if waving mother goodbye and setting off on a three-thousand mile
sea voyage was no more unusual than a game of croquet or a picnic
on the Sussex sands. In her autobiography, Vera Brittain calls the
children Hilary and Richard, probably thinking it inappropriate to
write openly about her own children. (However, Shirley Williams
told me herself recently: 'As far as I know, Richard and Hilary are
certainly meant to be my brother John and myself.')

Vera Brittain was lucky in having a job with CORB at the time,
and a posse of friends in the US eager to take in her children. She
settled for friends in the mid-West. An inner voice had told her not
to delay, that war had no concern for maternity and childhood, and
that if she wanted to save them, she had to pay the price of
separation. But it wasn't easy, as she confessed:

The morning so long dreaded has come. Last night I delayed as long as I could over drying Hilary's slim fairy-like body and brushing Richard's thick nut-brown hair. Sleepless, I looked at their sleeping faces – Richard's long dark eyelashes motionless on his cheeks, Hilary's fair serene face as unperturbed as an angel's. Modern children, endowed as though by some law of compensation with a calm emotional detachment which they cannot have inherited from their war-ridden parents of the Lost Generation, they neither fear nor even speculate about the adventure before them . . .

At the docks we are ushered into a large covered shed, to wait for what seem indefinite hours till the immigration officials arrive. Tired out already by the long train journey, the dozens of babies lift their voices one by one in loud wails of protest, and soon the dock resembles the parrot-house at the zoo . . .

A Canadian Pacific official approaches us.

'Are these the children who hold re-entry permits to the United States?'

Richard and Hilary move forward in proud assent . . .

A cold rainy wind blows suddenly over the docks. Beyond the enclosure we see now the grey-painted hulk of the anonymous liner, waiting to carry away from us the dearest possessions that are ours on earth. No – not our possessions. We never possessed them; they have always possessed themselves . . .

At the entrance to the gangway, they turn and wave cheerfully. Then the tarpaulin flaps behind them, and they are gone.

While Vera Brittain carries her ice-cold heart back to London and her busy, therapeutic job interviewing ships' escorts at CORB, near Piccadilly Circus, her desperately missed children continued their happy adventure ('like departing for a weekend visit to a familiar relative', their mother wrote ruefully). She finally heard of their safe arrival at the American port on the Eastern seaboard and then received a chirpy letter from Hilary-Shirley: 'The train journey only took us two days. In the train all the people were awfully friendly and gave us meals and iced drinks and sweets at their own expense. Indeed they kept coming one after another and didn't stop until the train did.' Merry children, being spoiled, sunk parents – this often constituted the overseas evacuation scenario.

One joyous trip for the 'Seavacs', as they came to be known, was the long, long voyage from Britain to Australia and New Zealand aboard the Polish ship, the *Batory*, in the summer of 1940. The Polish crew were charming, making light of it when they were chased by submarines. Also contributing to the fun was the eccentric and delightful CORB escort, Meta Maclean, who conducted the 500 Scottish, Welsh and English children in daily sessions of community singing. Singing characterized the voyage from start to finish. Geoffrey Shakespeare led the children in the singing of *There'll Always Be an England* at the Liverpool docks where they embarked in late July. The audience of grim parents had a moment of light relief when they realized that the children were fudging the word 'England' and making it 'Britain' – regional rivalry reared its head even at that tense moment. It turned out to be a marathon voyage, the ship stuffed to the gunwales with humanity, including 600 troops who were headed for Singapore. The ship, a luxury liner, called at Cape Town, Bombay, Colombo, Singapore, Fremantle, Melbourne and Sydney and apart from the children's seasickness and careless-ness with their gas masks (which they were required to hang near their bunks), it passed off happily.

The stop at Cape Town was particularly joyful as the weather was sparkling, the children relieved to have a four-day respite from mounting the waves, and the Cape Town residents wonderfully hos-pitable. Researching this moment in the Seavac history was fascinat-ing because I found so many happy references to the stopover from several different sources. Meta Maclean, the redoubtable escort who had the children singing nearly every day for the sixty days of the trip (culminating in the composition of their own song, *The Call*), described the visit in her book, aptly named, *The Singing Ship*:

> Each day spent at Cape Town brought increased pleasure and widening of experiences for the children. They were entertained at the picturesque home of the Governor-General where, after afternoon tea, they roamed with delight and wonder through the parks and gardens, trying to learn the name of every new flower and shrub. Some small boys and girls wandered hand-in-hand, like little Hansels and Gretels in fairyland, gazing with big eyes on these beautiful shore surroundings after their long time on the ocean.
>
> One thing that they found intensely interesting was the adjacent home of General Smuts. All of them, practically, mentioned in their next letters home having seen this house,

and that they had met, at picnics and other treats, members of the family of that famous patriot . . .

The people of Cape Town seemed to feel that nothing was too much for these storm-tossed waifs who had come from a war-torn country. At war with Germany too, the people of the Dominion often felt they were having it too easy, sheltered thousands of miles from the real action – entertaining evacuees was a way in which they could compensate for not doing anything more tangible to help. Not only did they entertain the Seavacs, they frequently took time to write each parent a personal letter telling them how their children were. Here is a letter written by a children's home director, Margaret Veitch, to Mrs Dorette Cuthbert of Stirling, Scotland about her two girls, Helen and Katherine, aged nine and seven:

> . . . they are dears and we loved them. They were the youngest allowed ashore, but the escort, the Scottish padre, knew lots of folk we knew and he was glad for Helen and Katherine to have the change. They both looked well . . .
>
> Helen had on her kilt and Katherine made it quite plain that she had one too, but there had been no time to change as they had only decided at the last minute to let her off.
>
> We do feel for you having to send them away, but the worst [for them] is over now and before you get this they will be landed.
>
> We have fruit-trees in the garden and [the] loquats were ripe; they enjoyed them as they did paw-paw in the fruit salad at lunch. In the afternoon we went down to the river to pick flowers. The arum lilies are just at their best. They picked masses to take back to their escorts on board . . .

Helen Cuthbert herself, resplendent in her kilt that day nearly fifty years ago, called her Cape Town visit a great 'highlight' when she told her story in *The Evacuees*. But she adored Australia, her final destination, even more. For her, to travel hopefully hadn't been a better thing than to arrive (to paraphrase R. L. Stevenson):

> And so began five very happy years for my sister and myself. We went to a large, good school; at first as day-girls, then, as my aunt got involved in war work, we became boarders. There were added excitements from our point of view (although not from that of our parents): there was a real scare in Australia that the Japanese might invade, so naturally it was thought

we had been sent out of the frying pan into the fire! Together
with our three cousins we were dispatched to a cattle station
for nine months to stay with some other relations. This was
marvellous for us. We had a small school on the property, so
our education was far from neglected. We learnt to ride,
and really learnt something of the 'outback'. We also had
marvellous holidays – beach holidays, with lots of surfing,
mountain holidays, on which we were taught to ski . . .

It is also interesting to read in Helen Cuthbert's account of her
life in Australia, that CORB officials used to come frequently to her
aunt's home in Sydney to find out how she was getting on. She says
they took her off to a separate room and 'asked lots of questions'.
It was unlikely that she was being abused by a close relation – and
of course she wasn't – but it is significant that the organization
continued to monitor the Seavacs' lives throughout their five-year
absence from Britain. In contrast, the occasional visits made by
billeting officers to the foster-homes of the home-based evacuees
seem a bit casual. But, of course, evacuees in rural billets in the
counties and shires of England were able to write complaining
letters home to readily available parents in the cities (and we know
that they did – regularly!) which, in itself, proved to be a safeguard
against abuse.

Ruth Fainlight, the poet, moved towards becoming an overseas
evacuee in several stages: the least memorable, she confesses, was
her year as an evacuee in Wales at the age of nine. She had travelled
there with her mother and brother from North London – three
blond, 'frail and in a way exotic' creatures. No one could fathom
them in their Welsh village, being baffled, she believes, by their
being evacuees from London and Jewish Londoners as well. This
was not the first time an evacuee, moved from a city to the country
in the Britain of fifty years ago, was made to feel altogether alien,
even a bit bizarre, for being Jewish (remember Mrs Kops* in
bucolic Nunmonkton!). Certainly Ruth and her family were made
to feel very keenly their 'apartness' from the Christian faith in
this tightly knit, dyed-in-the-wool Protestant community. Ruth
Fainlight half believes the Welsh villagers thought they were 'curing'
them of their Jewishness with Christmas presents and festivities –
seductive rites from a 'truer' faith. It was enough to make her feel
relieved when she learnt they were to escape to America (in mid-

*See Chapter 2, pp. 31–2.

1941 the three of them scrambled aboard the last refugee ship to leave Britain). Their New York-bound liner was to leave from Galway, and so Ruth and her brother and mother had to take a roundabout journey, with the Irish Sea crossing remaining most vividly in her mind. To get there:

> We crossed one night, sitting up in a garishly lit saloon and kept awake, delighted and rather frightened by a very drunk man who talked and sang for hours as the boat lurched and the floor tilted him back and forth, but never enough for him to fall down completely. His sallow features surrounded by dark, tossed hair were the liveliest thing I had seen for some time.

When they arrived in Galway, they found chaos: a crowded mail-room on the boat had been turned into dormitories for the mothers and children, and all the grown-ups were worriedly whispering about whether or not they would be torpedoed. They weren't, and Ruth felt 'a strong surge of emotion' when they sighted the Statue of Liberty in New York harbour. Looking back, Ruth Fainlight doubts the genuineness of many of the emotions she experienced then, including her delight at the Statue of Liberty, because as she admits, 'the violent change of everything called evacuation stunned me'.

Unlike Ruth, Bunty Buckland (now fifty-nine) did not feel like a 'leaf-in-the-wind' when she was told she would voyage alone to Canada on the *Volendam* in August 1940. It was something she longed to do. She was positively excited at the prospect of leaving her Redhill, Sussex home to live with her uncle, a vicar, in Toronto. He had whetted her desire to come to live in Canada by describing the lovely bedroom he and his family had decorated in readiness for her arrival. Perky, tiny, a bit of a tomboy, she was thrilled with the new wardrobe her mother had bought her for the trip. And she was also overjoyed to be one of the four children from the borough of Redhill and Reigate to be selected as overseas evacuees. She had no inkling then of the near disaster to come as she and 335 other children (320 of them with CORB, as was Bunty) set sail from Liverpool en route to New York on 28 August.

Bunty, formerly Mabel Harding, met me on a brilliantly sunny day in August 1987, near Haywards Heath where she now lives with her store-manager husband of forty years' standing. She is the grandmother of four small boys and remains a very attractive

woman. She would have been elected a Sussex beauty queen at
seventeen if she hadn't been so short – 5′1″ – she told me, good-
naturedly. The experience, at eleven, of nearly drowning, when the
Volendam was torpedoed and sank on 30 August 1940, has left her
unmarked. Indeed, the day I met her she was about to go sailing
off Shoreham at the weekend with her grown-up son, although she
still won't travel on a Hovercraft:

We got on the ship at Liverpool by which time I was the only
evacuee from Redhill and Reigate as the three others had been
sent back to Sussex. I don't know why. We were told that no
one knew when we had embarked as it was all secret in case
Hitler heard about it. That was why I could not say any
goodbyes at home. The only outsider who knew I was going,
apart from the family, was my headmaster. He gave me a book
to remember them all by and said he would tell the whole
school when I had arrived in Canada.

On board ship we were taken to our various cabins. I shared
mine with a twelve-year-old girl called Doreen who took the
upper bunk, which irritated me a bit, I remember. Our escort
was a very nice lady, a Canadian, who, I presume, was going
back home.

We duly unpacked our bits and pieces and I put my prize
possession, Bashful, one of the seven dwarfs from *Snow White
and the Seven Dwarfs* which I'd seen the year before, on the
porthole. We were then given life jackets, which we had to keep
on the whole time. They were like big pillows back and front.
We had lifeboat drill every day. When a bell rang, we all had
to congregate in our various groups and proceed to the library
where they gave us a talk on what we were to do if it happened
for real. It was a part of our daily lives and so by the third day,
we were quite used to hearing the bell ring and trouping off in
an orderly fashion.

It must have been about ten o'clock on the third day that
the bells started to ring. I noticed a funny smell and thought
something was different as there seemed to be a haze everywhere. We proceeded to the library and then were told to go
out on deck where it was very dark except for what appeared
to be torches flashing against the ship. Then they told us to go
back to the library and no sooner had we got there when there
was a commotion and I heard, 'Abandon ship!' and 'Take to

the lifeboats!' These were rowboats and we got into them and were lowered down into the dark waters. I do remember the ropes had to be cut and we landed with a plop. The sea was very rough. I remember thinking that if the ship sank I would lose all the new clothes I had and what a lot of hassle my mother would give me as a result.

After a half an hour, my boat was rescued by an oil tanker and I was shoved in a banana basket with two other girls and hauled up to a deck where a nice, grey-haired officer escorted me to his cabin. I got sick in his shaving bowl and I remember feeling very embarrassed by this, but the man was very nice about it.

The *Volendam* was struck by a German U-boat (U-60) at 22:00 GMT (Bunty was right) on Friday, 30 August. Considering the heavy load of passengers and crew she was carrying – a total of 606 in all – the fatalities were amazingly light – only two people were killed, the purser and a cabin-boy, a tragic loss but small in comparison to the disaster that overtook the passengers on the *City of Benares* seventeen days later. Three ships picked up the survivors: the *Valldemora*, a Norwegian freighter (Bunty's saviour), and two British tankers. Bunty was correct in thinking that the fact they were still wearing their life jackets full-time was partly responsible for their survival. She gives a little shudder when she recalls they were meant to take them off on the fourth day out – the day after the torpedoing – when it was presumed they would be out of the danger zone. The rest of her journey back to Britain is now hazy to her although she still remembers hordes of newspapermen greeting the children when they docked at Gourock, Scotland, on 1 September. A city official handed her a sprig of heather in welcome. It seemed a poor exchange for the suitcase of new clothes she had lost in the sinking (returned to her in Sussex months later), and when she arrived back in Redhill, her mother said she looked a 'pathetic little figure' with her carrier bag and peaky face. Returning was a frightful anti-climax, she confesses, but her parents tried to soften the blow by giving her a new kilt by way of consolation. Kilts, it seems, were prize possessions!

Bunty had a charmed life. Many of the CORB children from the *Volendam* did not go back home as she did, but waited in Liverpool for the next ship out, which was the ill-fated *City of Benares*.

Jack Keeley, a hopeful little evacuee like Bunty from southeast

England, walked up the gangplank to board the *City of Benares*. He turned out to be one of the thirteen children saved from what was the worst tragedy involving evacuees throughout the war, when seventy-seven children drowned in a cruel, icy sea, unseasonably wintry for the third week of September. Jack travelled, as Bunty had done, under the auspices of CORB. He was the sole CORB child survivor of the *Benares*; the other child survivors had sailed under the auspices of private agencies.

I met 57-year-old Jack Keeley on a stormy June night in 1987 at his small, terraced home in Tonbridge, Kent. A railway signalman for the past fifteen years, he is a big handsome man, over 6′ tall, twice-married with two grown children and a noisy collection of uncaged parrots, who strutted and screeched about our heads during the interview. Recently Jack had a heart by-pass operation, but he has obviously made a good recovery and was back at work in his responsible, high pressure job. He told his extraordinary story calmly, in an altogether relaxed fashion.

Jack was just nine when the bombing started over London in 1940, and his father, a retired soldier who had settled for the remainder of his life in Brixton, South London, decided to sign him up with CORB, eager to find a safe refuge for Jack and his younger sister, Joyce, aged six. They were children of older parents – their mother was fifty-two – and neither of them had travelled further than Skegness on school holidays. In their opinion they might just have been off to Mars as Canada:

I wasn't ready for a journey to Canada. Working-class families hardly ever travelled in those days and I was no exception. I had no idea of the implications of the trip. It was my 66-year-old Victorian father's idea. He was an ex-regular army man and a complete dictator in his own home. He'd been in the Boer War, the First World War – served in India and Africa, too – and well, I'm sure he'd become fearful of war after all this.

We took the train to Liverpool with two coachloads of children. We stayed at a school in Liverpool for two or three days before setting sail on the *City of Benares* at 6 p.m. on Friday the 13th. We knew we were headed for Canada, but we had no idea of the distance involved. The first days on the *Benares* struck us as being a huge lark. We had full waiter service and ad lib ice cream. You could say we were living off the fat of the boat! I've never been so drastically removed from one environment to another. Brixton was a hard life for poor people and we were certainly poor. It was coal fires and dirty coconut mats in front of the fire. We were happy as Larry on the ship, running around the decks, being taken care of by pretty college students. I thought it was an enormous ship, but I discovered later it was only eleven and a half thousand tons.

We had two destroyers with us for a period, until we crossed what was an imaginary line in the Atlantic after about three days out. On the fourth day a German submarine got under and up the middle of the ship. We were all in bed and there was a tremendous explosion. We'd had the boat drill so we got in our life boats. I was plummeted right into the water, which I didn't care for much, so when I saw a rope ladder I grabbed it and returned to deck, standing there frozen. I then felt myself being dragged off the deck – the *Benares* sank in thirty minutes – and was bobbing about in the water. My boots got lost and I thought 'What'll Father say?' I saw a raft with two men on it, an engineer and a BBC type, as it turned out.* I pulled myself on to the raft and the two men sat on me as I lay under them. It was the only way they could keep me on. I wasn't scared but my teeth were chattering like a German machine gun. The three of us seemed to be on that raft for an eternity.

We lived on some biscuits we found in a neat little cupboard. There was also some tinned milk and some water. But the twenty-foot waves kept sweeping things away. This is how we lost one of the four tins of milk. At one point, the engineer slipped off the raft and we eased him back on inch by inch. I felt fogged the whole time. It was rather like having the flu.

We were down to the last can of milk when we saw a warship. It was the HMS *Hurricane*, a wonderful sight after about forty-eight hours at sea. It took us back to Glasgow and we were there for four or five days. It was all a nightmare, but I don't know, it didn't quite sink in, any of it. My friends say it's made me quite a cynical person.

*The 'BBC type' Jack mentioned was Eric Davis, who survived to write about Jack in a *Reader's Digest* article published in January 1941. He wrote that Jack, 'who was wearing two life jackets but very little clothing' when they picked him up, was the soul of politeness. With teeth chattering like castanets, he managed to say: 'I say, thank you very much.' The men were charmed. Jack was a stocky, sturdy boy, Davis wrote, but even so he would have frozen if the two grown men hadn't spent many hours rubbing down his back, arms and legs.

One of the crucial things that 'never quite sank in' for many years – perhaps his mind had carefully insulated him in order to protect his strong, survivor spirit – was that his sister, Joyce, had drowned, probably just as he was being pulled aboard the raft. It wasn't until he returned to London and rejoined his desperate mother that Joyce's death penetrated his consciousness.

> Mother kept asking me about Joyce but I didn't know what to tell her. I was too busy worrying about the bombs that were beginning to rain down on us in Brixton, worse than the hailstones when we were bobbing around on that raft! I remember that some of them rumbled and others whistled when they came down. I was very happy to be evacuated to Macclesfield in the Midlands. I hated those bombs. This was three weeks after I was picked up at sea. I stayed with a well-off vicar and his family for three years and I had a pleasant enough time. But then, when I returned to Brixton finally, I got kind of wild. I wasn't the sort of juvenile that went around mugging or anything, but I was rather knockabout. I liked a drink or two. My father had passed away by then. In fact, he died shortly after the *Benares* went down.

The sinking of the *Benares* seems to have killed Jack's father from the shock of his daughter's drowning. It also sent shock waves reverberating across Britain. The *Benares*, which had been sunk 500 miles off the coast of Ireland, had been carrying 300 people, more than three-quarters of whom were drowned. It had been manned by a crew of Lashkars, 166 Indian crewmen, who were totally untrained in rescue operations and, in any event, could not understand the Captain's orders emanating from the loudspeaker, as they had no English. The ship had been carrying too many passengers, an inquiry revealed later, and of the twelve lifeboats launched, only one had been dry. Bad weather set in soon after the lifeboats were put overboard, and many children ended up sitting waist-deep in icy water. In retrospect, it seemed remarkable that as many as seventeen children survived.

Its sinking also sank the CORB programme, although the nation was sympathetic and funds poured into the organization. The Germans denied having torpedoed the ship, a denial no one believed, for good reason. Geoffrey Shakespeare suggested that future evacuee ships should be fast ships (the *City of Benares* had been steaming along slowly when it was struck); adequately convoyed by warships;

and manned by English-speaking crews. However, his suggestions seemed ambitious, especially since winter in the North Atlantic was approaching with its attendant rough seas and foul weather conditions. The Prime Minister and the Admiralty, both of whom had disapproved of the scheme in the first place, continued to express their disapproval with renewed vigour after the *Benares'* tragedy. As a result, and with a sad inevitability, CORB ceased to operate after October 1940, causing the 200,000 mothers and children still remaining on the organization's waiting list grave disappointment. Evacuees continued to set sail after the disaster of 17 September but not in the same numbers and through the efforts of small private committees formed to assist them. By late 1941, they, too, stopped sending evacuees abroad.

But, throughout the autumn of 1940, children disembarked in large parties on to the New York piers, both before the *Benares* went down and during the month which followed. Press attention was at its most feverish after the sinking, naturally enough, and interviews with the children filled the pages of the *New York Times* during the first week of October.

The three states in America which were the most welcoming to the evacuees were Massachusetts, New York and Ohio. Massachusetts was influenced by its long colonial history and the strong pro-British political stance of those of its citizens claiming English ancestry (this did not apply to its Irish immigrant population whose ties were then, as now, with the Irish Republic, which was neutral throughout World War II); New York, traditionally, was a centre of internationalism and noted for the philanthropy of its more affluent citizens; Ohio responded to the plight of the evacuees because of the highly industrialized nature of the state, and the appreciation felt by Ohioans for the many British workers who had previously immigrated there and had proved themselves able and industrious.

However, these three states, while taking the largest proportion of evacuees, were by no means their exclusive hosts. Sympathy for Britain's plight spilled over to include its children and such high profile groups as Warner Brothers, and firms like Eastman Kodak in Rochester, New York, were among the many wealthy companies to succour them. (Warner Brothers in California, for example, sponsored a large group of British children who arrived on the *Scythia* on 3 October 1940.) The evacuees were sponsored by these huge businesses and then farmed out to the families of those who worked for them. As we know, the initial spurt of compassion generated for the evacuees in America, while genuine, did become less fervid as the war progressed and rationing, the draft, and war casualties overseas hit the US itself. But while America was neutral and Britain's back was against the wall – as it most assuredly was in the autumn of 1940 – American pity, to the point of sentimentality, enveloped them.

The uncertainty surrounding the overseas evacuation programme permeates the following *New York Times* report of 4 October 1940, and reveals how hedged with secrecy and apprehension the trips had become. It also demonstrates the degree to which the British children had captured American hearts:

> The first large group of refugee British children to come direct to New York in more than a month arrived here yesterday on three British liners, the Cunard White Star liners, *Scythia* and *Samaria* and the Furness cargo passenger liner *Western Prince*.
>
> There were more than 500 children in all, approximately 250 each on the two larger vessels and 37 on the *Western Prince*. Although none of the ships' officers would discuss their voyage in detail it was evident from the talk of the less inhibited youngsters that the three vessels had come most of the way in convoy, probably the same one.
>
> Representatives of the United States Committee for the Care of European Children went down the bay carrying newspapers that announced Britain's decision to stop the evacuation of child refugees, and officials of the group said that this was probably the last big one.

The *Scythia* children, aged five to fifteen, were very chirpy according to the newspaper, and when they weren't racing cheerfully all over the decks, would join in singing heart-tugging songs about their own status. Led by the conductor of the ship's orchestra, they sang one for the newspapermen, which the *New York Times* reporter described:

> They were a gay group . . . and all of them seemed to face the strange future in an alien land with the same self-possession displayed by the hundreds of children who have preceded them here.
>
> As the ship moved up the bay, they gathered on the canvas-covered forward hatch and turned the thumbs up in the gesture

that now typifies British hope and determination . . . They stood together and sang a song taught to them on the way over by Bert Binks, the ship orchestra leader . . . and charged headlong through such phrases as 'let the world see that the youth of Britain stands the test' and ending up on a plaintive note, 'We are the Seaevacuees, waiting for the message "all clear, come home please."''

One interview the reporter had with a London thirteen year old, Nigel Fletcher, proved how unprepared the children were for their American homes. He said that his father, Stanley, who worked in the catering trade, had just pointed a finger at the map of the United States, remembered that he had a friend from World War I in White Plains, and decided that that would be the destination of Nigel and his two younger sisters, Jacqueline, six, and Patricia, ten. So, the three children were heading for upstate New York, its impending winter snows, and a city in which a vague friend of their father's had once lived (it was not, however, his friend to whom they were going!). Perhaps because the children were coming to the potentially sub-zero winter weather of the US Eastern seaboard, from a damp, but milder, climate, the Red Cross was waiting at the Cunard Line pier with 'sweaters, mufflers and caps'. With cosy hospitality, it also provided them with hot chocolate, tea and 'biscuits', explaining that these were called 'cookies' in America. For the children this was just the beginning of an extensive overhaul of their language and customs.

Taken to sightsee on a bus trip round Manhattan, eighty of the new arrivals 'from London, Oxford, Kent and Surrey, Devon, Hampshire and Lancashire', who had been lodging at the Seamen's Church Institute under the auspices of the US Committee for the Care of European Children, pronounced themselves unimpressed with the New York 'tubes'. They were not as fast and comfortable as London's, the children announced. We call it a 'subway', said their bus driver indulgently, ignoring the invidious civic comparison. When shown Grant's Tomb, one eleven-year-old boy from Surrey said, 'Who is this chap, Grant, anyway?' An eight-year-old girl from London admitted she was happy to see traffic again, and a gracious ten-year-old boy from Liverpool confessed he thought the New York taxi drivers were more efficient and faster than the ones he'd seen back home. Times Square and Broadway were the biggest hits because most of the older children had seen them in films.

Anglo-American differences provided the children with giggles and exclamations in their first few days in America, all of which were carefully reported in the press. The children had never seen showers before, they said, and so piled into the seamen's shower rooms at the Institute to enjoy the novelty of gushing water overhead. They astounded their adult escorts by rising at dawn (6 a.m.!), earlier than American children did, and asking for tea instead of milk (they got milk, like it or not). They tried to make sandwiches out of the 'loose' eggs in their sauceboat-sized cups ('Where are the egg cups?' they wanted to know). Homesickness was only painfully apparent on a few occasions, when, as the columnist put it 'some of the smaller children became lonesome and obtained permission to crawl into bed with older brothers and sisters'.

Nearly a week after the children had arrived on the Cunard liners, the newspapers were still able to milk winsome feature stories from their activities. On 8 October 1940 a *New York Times* report headed 'British Boys Get Baseball Lesson', described this cross-cultural venture:

Under the critical and finally approving eyes of neighbourhood children, nineteen English refugee boys took to the American pastime of baseball yesterday at the Columbus playground, just off Foley Square.

The boys, ranging in age from eight to fifteen, were part of the group of more than one hundred children being quartered at the Seamen's Church Institute . . . Most arrived in America last Thursday aboard the British liners *Samaria* and *Scythia*.

Carmine Caruccio, a volunteer worker with the Committee for the Care of European Children, undertook the task of explaining the intricacies of the game to the boys, who then took the field to play an informal practice game. No score was kept.

With American youngsters on the sidelines yelling encouragement on the first batters, twelve-year-old John Cushen of Bromley, Kent, made his a home run. Later, he added two more to become the hitting star of the day. 'Gosh, he looks like Joe DiMaggio' one of the spectators commented.

Their jolly New York introduction to America lasted from three days to just under a week, depending on the connections the children were making. And New York wasn't all baseball games and sightseeing tours, either. All the children were subjected to gruelling medical examinations before they could be given the all-clear to travel further inland. It was just as well they had this period of adjustment because many of the subsequent train rides were over-long, unbroken and exhausting. All evacuees who disembarked at Halifax, Nova Scotia, for example, en route for Canadian foster-homes had to undergo an uncomfortable rail journey. A *New York Times* story of 6 October, described one such trip:

> Following their arrival at Halifax, there was a twenty-seven hour trip by rail to Montreal in a train used for transporting soldiers, on which many of the children slept on boards and without blankets. Throughout all this Miss Kuhn [their committee escort] said the children's spirits had been unusually high.

The children kept their memories of wartime Britain fresh by carrying grim mementoes with them, the *New York Times* correspondent related:

> Nearly all the young evacuees . . . carried gas masks as well as fragments of bombs and Nazi warplanes as souvenirs. Many had breathless tales to tell of bombs that landed near their homes. Bruce and Roderick Cargill of Buckminster Gate,* London, whose home was shattered by a 300-pound bomb that passed through the roof and exploded in the cellar, said they were going to stay [in North America] for the duration.

Margaret Hanton, fifty-six, mother of three, and a pre-school playgroup volunteer worker living in Dulwich, southeast London, may easily have been one of the high-spirited evacuees en route to a foster-home in Canada which the newspaper described. She arrived in North America in July 1940, aged eight, after having had a wonderful time on board ship, playing cards with a group of lumberjacks returning home and avoiding her rather serious fourteen-year-old brother. Margaret's parents were academics, her father a lecturer at Birmingham University and her mother a teacher who taught Margaret at home. Margaret was extremely advanced academically – she entered Girton College, Cambridge at the end of the war – and her seven-year stay in Toronto began oddly for her when she entered the sixth-grade, three years younger than any of her classmates:

*A reporter's error, I think, it was probably Buckingham Gate.

I was quite surprised by my foster-parents: they seemed a tremendous age – in their fifties and old enough to be my grandparents. In those days, there weren't any mid-Atlantic people. You were either Canadian or American – rarely British. This couple was extremely pro-British but they didn't know any British people. My funny accent was noted by them and by almost everyone, but most people were very emotional about what was happening back in Britain – the war – and so they made a fuss of me.

I wasn't homesick at all, at first, and then it began to hit me. I felt bereaved. Intellectually I knew my parents cared for me, but emotionally I felt they'd abandoned me. There was nothing to show that they cared – no telephone calls in those days, of course, and letters took three weeks. You'd write them about a fireworks party you'd been to and it would be long over by the time they wrote you back commenting on it. I had a permanent guilt complex about not writing them enough. But it was as if they had died.

Their standards were different from my family's. I found it distressing that my foster-mother would do something that my mother wouldn't have done. She had her hair permed and she wore lipstick. She wanted me to wear shoes all the time whereas at home I'd been told that shoes scuffed floors and that I should wear slippers in the house. My foster-mother wanted me to be 'pretty-pretty', but my mother had not approved of my being vain. In the end, she gave up on trying to prettify me and let me be an intellectual. My foster-father was a college lecturer and took pride in the fact that I was clever and he won the battle.

I didn't feel I was in the way. I was very anxious to please. I wasn't secure enough to be bad. My foster-mother used to tease me and say, 'If you don't behave, I'll send you back to St George Street.' That had been the reception centre. I believed her. My brother was with a family on the same street but I didn't see much of him. He was so much older than me that it was difficult for us to be close. I think his adaptation was very much more difficult than mine at first. In the end he did convert totally to the Canadian way of life, but it took him longer. He's lived there ever since.

My mother came over in 1946 and I think she probably shocked me. By that time, my accent was so Canadian that I couldn't convince people I'd originally come from England. She was insensitive to North American manners and she wasn't dressed like other people. She was saddened because she felt no one there was interested in what Britain had gone through during the war, but of course they didn't want to hear about this all the time. They just wanted to show her the beauties and wonders of Southern Ontario and were hurt by her dismissal of Canadian things. Here she was in a conventional, middle-class, professional Canadian home with a daughter who had turned into a little conformist. She embarrassed me. I wanted to remain Canadian and was totally loyal to the Canadian outlook. I must have been quite a bundle of conflicts when she took me back to England at fifteen. I adjusted back to British ways, largely because I preferred schooling in England, but you couldn't say I was a happy teenager. Happiness didn't come until my maturity. In a way, I had to grow up when I was eight.

Margaret Hanton's foster-parents may have been a bit provincial, but there is no doubting their kindness. They took her to their hearts and even tried to extend their warmth towards her prickly mother. It's probably fair to say that it was easier to deal with an evacuee when the child was unaccompanied by a proud, stubborn parent who wished to discuss the deprivations of war-torn Britain!

One of the unavoidable awkwardnesses arising from the North American evacuation was that the Canadian and American hosts were often so much wealthier than their young guests. Returning from a vast home in Dayton, Ohio, after his boyhood evacuation, Anthony Bailey said he found everything in his parents' bungalow in Southampton 'closer, denser, more tangible'.* He felt like Gulliver in Lilliput, everlastingly trying not to bump into things (changes in the size of their environments also shocked British evacuees returning from rural homes to town semis, as my interview with Stan Clater in the last chapter indicates).

Currency restrictions prevented fathers, remaining in England, from buying and sending dollars to their families when their wives and children were evacuated overseas. As a consequence, the evacuees and their financially pressed mothers often felt like 'poor cousins' in their new homes, as Elizabeth Forsyth remarked in *The Evacuees*:

*See Chapter 9, pp. 150–1.

... he [her father] was unable to supply us with any money at all. So my mother depended on Toronto friends, first very modestly to furnish our apartment, and then to clothe and feed us all for four years, friends kindly willing to take the chance of my father being alive and able to repay them when the war was over ... My mother reminds me that the total spent on furnishing, including kitchen and other equipment, was only £25, and we slept on mattresses which cost but ten shillings each, with pillows which cost one shilling. I, for one, do not remember being any the worse for it.

There were considerable differences in food ... Even at the age of six I was impressed by the fact that the can-opening – pardon me, I should say the tin-opening – craze which had not hit England very considerably then ... was already in full blast on the other side of the Atlantic.

It was difficult, if not impossible, for even the more comfortably off British children to forget that they were often living on charity in their North American billets. Others forgot to expect creature comforts they had known at home. My older sister, Anne Magill, remembers two very pretty, aristocratic, English teenagers at Wellesley College outside Boston, which she attended in 1941, putting their shoes out to be shined in the dormitory halls. After a few days, they realized their gaffe. Many evacuees told me they learned cultural differences by making a series of similar *faux pas*. Their American hosts were good-natured, at least, and their mistakes never earned them lasting opprobrium.

What to do with one's accent was often a vexed question for an evacuee. Did one keep it, modify it or lose it altogether – many possibilities presented themselves. Margaret Hanton admitted she shed hers in Toronto since she wanted to conform and was ashamed of her mother's strong, 'teacherish' and obviously upper-class accent when she came to retrieve her daughter six years after her arrival in Canada. Others clung to theirs for years – it was their badge of identity, proof of their individuality, and of their loyalty to the brave country they had left behind.

Elizabeth Ogg, the *New York Times* feature writer mentioned on p. 107, recounted the following story of how one little girl coped with the matter of accent, in her post-war report of the evacuees who had settled back in Britain:

The question of 'accents' was always coming up in connection with evacuating English children to the United States. Out of homesickness and an exaggerated sense of loyalty to their native land, some of the evacuees over-emphasised their British speech and manners and became super-British. One such little girl maintained this pose throughout her stay in America, but as soon as she returned to England dropped her clipped speech almost completely and became a vociferous defender of things American.

Obviously, when your accent is not taken for granted, it can become something you can make a conscious decision to lose or keep and actually burnish. It was a precocious choice for a youngster to have to make. One evacuee, Jeremy Thorpe, decided to keep his while showing how adept he was at mimicking others at the same time. Jeremy, aged eleven in 1940, was dispatched to Connecticut, where he attended the Rectory School and, according to the biography, *Jeremy Thorpe: A Secret Life*, he shone:

> . . . amongst the forty or so pupils Jeremy made an immediate impression. He was already a self-confident and precocious boy, clever, witty, more popular perhaps with teachers than with fellow-pupils, good àt French, more than proficient at the violin, a good actor and a budding public speaker. His gift for mimicry was already developing, and he was able to pick up a deep southern American accent which is by far the hardest to imitate well . . . Thorpe himself claims to have picked up his first radical inclinations as a reaction to the Republicans with whom he found himself in contact at his aunt's house. 'Perhaps it was the sheer cussedness of a child,' he said later, 'or because I couldn't stand Republicans. But I went around sticking Roosevelt pins on them all.' It was certainly true that by the time he returned to England – in 1943, aboard a destroyer – he was sufficiently changed to resent the discipline of Eton, the school to which he was now sent.

It is easy to see here, in the adventures of this young Connecticut evacuee, intimations of his brilliant career as a Liberal politician in adulthood; a career cut short in full bloom in 1979 by his alleged homosexual association with the male model Norman Scott. One thing the young Thorpe proved was that an evacuee to North America need not lose his national identity. Not changing your style or your identify to fit in with a new environment takes courage.

Lallie Didham, née Lallie Lee Lowis, was an evacuee who attended Dana Hall, an expensive girls' day and boarding school in Wellesley, Massachusetts; later she married a gentleman farmer and lived in Kenya for thirty-six years. She said she took a conscious decision to keep her accent. We talked about it in London in the summer of 1987 while she was here from Africa for Ascot:

> I was twelve when we were evacuated from Britain and I wasn't really cut off from my family. My father was English but my mother was American and my grandmother lived in Boston so it was logical that we should be evacuated there. I came to America with my two sisters and brother and New England looked very good to me. I liked the friendliness of the American girls at Tenacre [the junior school] and later at Dana Hall, which was a paradise compared to the British boarding school I'd been attending. I kept my accent. I'm not very musical so didn't pick up the American intonation, and an English accent was an asset on the whole.

Lallie Didham decided that her accent was an 'asset' and kept it (she still has it today, in late middle-age, after so many years spent in Africa).

At Dana Hall, she was plunged into a different social setting than she had known in England; she gritted her teeth and carried off her new life with aplomb. (Many girl evacuees, in particular, found American dating habits and social behaviour more precocious – and therefore more bewildering – than what they were familiar with at home. This is probably not the case today since British teenagers also 'go steady', spend Saturday nights at the disco, attend pop concerts, drink Tequila Sunrises and smoke behind their parents' backs and wear expensive gear. But during the war, there was no teenage cult to speak of in Britain.) Lallie Didham thinks her over-sophisticated life as an evacuee left some odd residues in her subsequent social behaviour:

> My life was far from run-of-the-mill in America. I was escorted around chic New York dances, went to night clubs – and this at about fifteen! I went to debbie dances in Newport, Rhode Island, and thought nothing about going to El Morocco or the '21' Club in Manhattan. Eventually, I 'came out', as they say, at a debutante ball with Jackie O. in Boston.
>
> What it did was to help me build a tremendous façade. I

developed an outward self-assurance that had nothing to do with the shy creature within. Here I was in this glittering society but my parents had no money, at least not during the war. Well, that was one good thing. It prevented me from becoming money-minded. But it's had the effect of making me very abrupt in social circles. I can't go into a strange room or a cocktail party today without attaching myself to a close friend or else I feel at sea. I lack confidence and I'm sure this is a direct result of my war experience.

Lallie's words were significant, I thought when we spoke, because until then most of my interviewees had concentrated on the details of their evacuation (what they could remember of it) and not of the impact the experience had had on their personalities. It occurred to me that a good deal of unconscious repression had been at work in their psyches as children, and that perhaps it had been less disturbing for them later in life to focus on the facts of their experiences rather than their effects. When, however, they did attempt, as adults, to dredge their childhood memories to dovetail long-ago events with some of the personal characteristics they possess today, they found potent links between the two which I will discuss in my final chapter.

But their ability to sit back and reflect, however superficially, on the effects of separation from home and family during evacuation did not arise until long after the event. The war dragged on interminably. By 1944, even the parents were beginning to wonder if their children would ever come home again. Just as they were contemplating a happy reunion, the third and last and – in a way – cruellest exodus came about, that of the 'Flying Bombs' Evacuation.

The Flying Bombs of 1944 and 1945: The Third and Final Evacuation

In the summer of 1944 London began to breathe again. The most battered of all Britain's cities, with the exception of Coventry, had seen no consistent blitzing for three years, although there had been intermittent bombing. Citizens of the East End, the most pock-marked, bomb-pitted and blitz-ravaged of the city's districts, were beginning to wake up after an infernal period of darkness, like Rip Van Winkles, to rub their eyes in the belief they were going to see the light again. The most cheering thought of all animating the majority of parents was that their evacuated children would soon come home for good! Or so they so longingly hoped . . . and they had good reason to do so.

The Ministry of Health had been formulating plans for the return of evacuees to their homes the year before, submitting its final report in December 1943. The exercise was by no means uncomplicated. For example, the 708 evacuees from Ealing, Middlesex, (as it was during the war before its transformation into London W13) were to be transported home from such diverse places as Penzance, Cornwall in the far southwest, and from points as far north as Halifax, Yorkshire and the Lancastrian towns further afield such as Burnley and Morecambe. Reading newspaper reports that such plans were in the pipeline, London parents quite naturally assumed there was a justifiable basis for optimism.

Then on 13 June 1944, at 4:25 a.m., came the nastiest surprise of the entire war in many Londoners' estimation – the first explosion of a new, German terror weapon, the V-1. These were rockets launched by the German Air Force from the Pas de Calais in France, pilotless planes which drifted over the southeast and the capital, before cutting out and exploding on impact. The first V-1 rocket exploded in Grove Road, Bow, early on this June morning and was shortly followed by five more, one harmlessly falling in the Channel and three others igniting in the fields of Kent.

Londoners were totally baffled by this bizarre new terror. They had wearily become inured to the unending bombing of the 'conventional' Luftwaffe type, which caused destruction from fires set alight by the incendiary bombs (as exemplified, most memorably, by the flaming dome of St Paul's during the night of 29 December 1940, when it was hit and unforgettably photographed for posterity), but they were not prepared for the innovative horror of the 'doodlebugs', as they soon became called. With the doodlebugs or buzz bombs, their other colloquial name, destruction and injury were almost entirely caused by bomb blast. Windows shattered and flying glass became lethal for anyone unfortunate enough to be within striking distance – and the distance could be up to a quarter of a mile's radius from the point of impact, depending on the size of the bomb's explosives. Victims were lacerated, often gruesomely wounded, when not killed outright.

The fear provoked by these weapons amongst the public was not dissipated by the machinations of the British High Command who tried to keep their appearance secret, both at home and abroad. For the first three days, Herbert Morrison, the Minister for Home Security, said nothing, not deigning to enlighten the people with an explanation of their composition nor of what to expect. Rumours sprang up, grew and multiplied all over London and the southeast. The most persistent rumour had it that the missiles were really German raiders shot down out of the skies. Curiously enough, this rumour was more comforting for some than the reality presented by the pilotless planes. Through a strange psychological quirk, it was later established that most people could 'accept' terror dealt out directly by another human being. What they found most terrifying about the buzz bombs was their revolutionary technology that dispensed with a flesh-and-blood airman and yet could rain destruction down upon them.

Herbert Morrison couldn't sustain his silence after the first few
days in mid-June, even though he felt it unwise to let the German
High Command realize exactly how successful it had been in
lowering morale in the capital. By 16 June the doodlebugs were
criss-crossing the skies at the rate of seventy-three a day. Reluc-
tantly, on that same day, the Minister announced the city was now
being attacked by pilotless planes. He continued to soft-pedal as
to their real destructive capacity, however, not wishing to make
Londoners abandon hope.

Some historians believe that the secrecy surrounding the V-1s
was so carefully constructed and, to a great degree, maintained in
Britain, it has obscured many facts about this strange episode right
up to the present day. In their recent book about London at war,
The Making of Modern London 1939–1945, Joanna Mack and Steve
Humphries write:

> In fact, Londoners have still not been told the whole truth
> about what really happened in this final attack on the capital.
> The scale of devastation and demoralization caused by the
> flying bombs was hushed up at the time in order to maintain
> morale. The secrets of London's ordeal were locked away in
> government files. Now that these records have been opened to
> the public, they reveal that during the last nine months of the
> war, London and its inhabitants faced a supreme challenge . . .
> This challenge came when Londoners were ill-equipped to face
> renewed suffering. They were tired and exhausted from
> five long years of war. Moreover, most people had believed
> that the landings in France would bring more or less instant
> victory.

While deliberate obfuscation as to their nature was being per-
petrated by Whitehall, confused and bitter quarrelling of an unedify-
ing kind flared up amongst the Allied High Command over the
missiles too. Considering that this should have been a period of
self-congratulation and jubilation within the Allied ranks – the
Normandy landing on D-Day, 6 June, a week before the first V-1
exploded in London, had been a success, with 156,000 British and
American troops reaching France – one has grimly to admit that
the Nazis got their own back with a vengeance (in fact, the rockets
were dubbed *Vergeltungswaffen*, 'vengeance weapons' by the German
military leaders). The rockets did, indeed, divide the Allied High
Command and demoralize the population of southeast England:

perhaps they were the last sting in the tail of a dying aggressor, but they successfully injected the slow poison of despair into the exhausted population of Great Britain.

The most bitter wrangle concerning how best to handle the new threat broke out between Churchill and Eisenhower: Churchill wanted the American Chief of Staff to threaten the Germans with the use of mustard gas in counter-retaliation for the rocket raids. General Eisenhower greeted his proposal with angry impatience. 'Let's, for God's sake, keep our eyes on the ball and use some sense,' he snapped.*

But the missile attacks on Britain's south-coast ports and on London and its environs had Eisenhower deeply worried. Dismissing Churchill's suggestion out of hand, he nonetheless decided to give first priority to dealing with them by mounting air attacks on the V-1 launch sites, an operation known within Bomber Command as CROSSBOW. As John Terraine writes in his book, *The Right of the Line,*

> the sites were difficult, elusive and unrewarding targets for any type of aircraft (as were those of the V-2 rockets which were known to be in preparation); in all some 3000 Allied aircrew would lose their lives in CROSSBOW operations.

As it turned out, the best counter-attack weapons against doodle-bugs were anti-aircraft guns. But the most satisfactory method of neutralizing the threat altogether remained the capture of their Pas de Calais launch sites by land. In nine months' time this was done, but the entire operation consumed about 50 per cent of the energies of Bomber Command. The nuisance and headache value represented by these rockets for the Allies cannot be underestimated.

Apart from their drain on Allied military resources and their demoralizing effect on the population, the rockets damaged property and killed people with alarming thoroughness. At the peak of the V-1 attacks 20,000 houses a day were damaged in London and its suburbs. Kent, the county which came to be known as 'Bomb Alley', was treated to the spectacle of skies filled with rockets both night and day. The skies over Sussex were alive with them, too. Croydon, now a staid and quite comfortable if sleepy suburb of South London, had a wild and bitter time with an incredible 142

*From Lord Tedder's book, *With Prejudice*.

buzz bombs exploding over it between June 1944 and March 1945. Sometimes the rockets' aim seemed diabolically accurate: this was the case on 18 June, five days after the V-1 raids began, when a direct hit destroyed the Guards Chapel in Central London, killing 119 people and badly injuring a further 102.

Not that the missile attacks were confined solely to London and the southeast; they penetrated as far away as Yorkshire and Nottinghamshire, but in general constituted a Greater London nightmare. When the more technologically advanced rockets, the V-2s, appeared in September, Londoners could not believe their ill-fortune. These were larger than the V-1s, forty-five feet long and weighing fourteen tons. They created small craters wherever they landed, and fell haphazardly from Chiswick on the far west of London to Epping at its eastern tip; only eight hit London but they created some disturbingly big holes in the capital.

Herbert Morrison hastened to open up the deeper tube shelters. This time, the underground havens were organized more safely than they had been during the blitzes of 1940–1. Only the deeper, safer ones were used and people had to buy tickets to enter them, which meant no overcrowding took place. Many exhausted Londoners, their nerves shattered from five years of war, went into the shelters and simply stayed there for the ten months of rocket attack, emerging only to do their daytime jobs.

But, in spite of such precautions and the extensive use of the shelters, thousands of civilians were maimed and killed. Chilling statistics record a total of 9000 people killed and 22,000 injured in the 'flying bombs' period, mostly in the Greater London area.

What the Ministry of Health did with its evacuation plans at this time revealed tremendous *sang-froid*. Instead of scrapping them entirely, it went on with its provincial plans and merely placed London at the back of the 'return' queue after realizing that the rockets would primarily affect London. As a result, in 1944–5 a strange contradictory evacuation scheme developed: provincial evacuees returned to their homes in Manchester, Birmingham, Liverpool and other cities, while a whole tribe of evacuees poured out of London to 'safe' billets in the countryside. In 1944 over a million women, children, elderly and disabled people were evacuated from the capital. Evacuation was a very checkered affair this time – only one in five people were officially evacuated by means of 'assisted evacuation' schemes (with government financial aid to a designated billet). The Third Evacuation contained much of the same feelings of panic and feisty individuality of the trekker era of 1940–1.

In many cases, in 1944 and 1945, London evacuees returned to billets they had been to before. By then, blessedly, many of the frictions and stresses that had arisen previously between evacuee mothers and their children, and their billeting hosts, had been ironed out. Also, the flying bombs were so terrifying and treacherous, their effects so lacerating and vile, that foster-parents became increasingly altruistic throughout this period. Certainly none of the ennui registered during the First Evacuation, with its feeling of purposelessness, seemed to develop. If not welcomed back with joy – after all, owing to the attritional rationing, it was yet more difficult in 1944 than ever before to produce decent meals for growing children – at least they *were* welcome.

Foster-parents knew how ghastly the rockets were from reading of the nastiness of the wounds inflicted by rocket blasts. Barbara Nixon, an Air Raid Warden in 1944, gave this example of one incident:

> Night or day you could usually see them coming, and hear the cut-out just before it dropped. If you lay flat on the ground you were probably safe at even only six or seven yards. They all had an impact fuse, and therefore although they blew in countless façades or backs of buildings, they did not bring down whole edifices. There were, of course, unlucky exceptions. One cut-out over the river, just cleared Bush House and fell in the Aldwych just as the streets were full of office workers hurrying to try to get some lunch. One of our wardens, who worked in the area, got caught in that one and was taken to hospital. He returned to our post in the evening after they extracted the object which had been blown into his leg – it was a button.

Even a button could become a small missile of supreme violence!

Newspaper reports describing the freakish bomb blasts did nothing to calm the public's nerves. As the suburbs became front-line targets, housewives in the modest semis and terraces of Chiswick, Ealing, Epping and Ilford became, understandably, panic-stricken. Today's suburban housewife may wilt in isolation, bemoaning unrealized dreams amid piles of unwashed saucepans. In 1944 her

self-same isolation meant that the nervous housewife faced possible
extinction alone with only her child or children for company. It has
been said that many housewives confused the sounds of their own
vacuum cleaners with the spluttering and buzzing of the V-1s.
Gurgling taps and the sound of frying sausages could also mimic
their noise. As a consequence, many women lived in a state of daily
auditory hell.

Brenda Bancroft, who had been evacuated to Oxfordshire during
the early 1940s (see Chapter 6, pp. 93–4), found herself living with
her grandmother in the West End of London in the summer of
1944, harrowed by both the sound of the V-1s and, worse still, the
lack of sound. As she told me:

> I was staying with my grandmother in her flat in Portman
> Square on my summer holiday. A rich widow, she was lonely
> and in any case, I think she thought I was becoming a bit too
> thick with my lovely Oxfordshire family. I was about twelve
> then and she was planning to send me to boarding school in
> the country in September – she must have thought this was
> going to keep me safe enough but then she hadn't bargained
> for the arrival of the buzz bombs.
>
> I heard the buzz bombs twice that summer. They made this
> awful click-click sound in the skies as they went over. It was
> the silence when they cut out I remember most vividly. I truly
> learned the significance of the term, 'pregnant silence'. Can
> you believe me when I talk about the 'sound of silence'? But
> this is what it was. I'd count until I heard the blast and the
> counting seemed interminable.
>
> As it was, my grandmother's building – she lived over the
> old children's school outfitters, Daniel Neal – was badly rocked
> when Selfridges was hit by a rocket later on. Her windows were
> blown in. She was relieved I was away at boarding school, she
> said. So was I.

Brenda Bancroft was more privileged than most evacuees, at least
materially, but her experience was typical in one way. By 1944, in
company with thousands of other children, she was beginning to
feel like a yo-yo. She had been dragged back from a happy billet to
spend a tedious and frightening summer with her grandmother,
and then shunted out to an unknown (to her) boarding school to
be kept safe once again. She had made one adjustment at nine years
of age and made it well, loving her foster-family, and now three

years later was supposed to fit in with her capricious grandmother's new plans for her.

And by 1944, most London evacuees, like Brenda, were beginning to feel as dizzy as human shuttlecocks. Many of them had been sent off in the Phoney War of 1939, brought back for the Christmases and New Years of 1939 and 1940, sent off again during the blitz years of 1940–1, recalled again in 1943, and then, when it was least expected, evacuated back to the rural areas once more in 1944.

But, of course, not all the 1944 evacuees were veterans of the experience like Brenda Bancroft. For thousands of very young children, it was their first taste of separation from home. Penny Tweedie, noted international photo-journalist, for example, was four years old when the buzz bombs crashed around her parents' home in June 1944. They lived in Esher, Surrey, which, like Croydon, its twin Southwest London suburb, became a frequent target of the missiles since they often cut out before reaching Central London. Her mother, a teacher with an infant son as well as Penny, decided that she would evacuate Penny to a privately-run boarding house.

Her private billet was in Gorleston on Sea, Norfolk, and Penny, a petite blonde child, stayed there for the nine months that the bombs continued to rain down over London, finally leaving when she was five. She is sure that she was too young to be evacuated without her mother, and remembers her experience with extreme distaste, her nose wrinkling as she recalls one menu in particular:

> The doodlebugs were terrifying, naturally. I can remember them vividly and the horrible noises they made. They crashed around in hot mid-summer.
>
> My mother acted quickly and sent me off to Norfolk to the home of a former governess she'd known. I can't remember whether she took me there, but I suppose she must have done. Then she returned to London. Anyway, I certainly felt abandoned. The first day I was there I was given a lunch of brains and cabbage. I couldn't swallow it. The former governess just took the dish away and offered it to me again for tea – all congealed by then. I refused again. As I was creating a 'fuss', as she saw it, I was treated as a particularly naughty child. For the first time, I was labelled as difficult.

Going to bed at night was no comfort because I was sharing
a room with an older girl, a Down's Syndrome child. She was
very restless and made funny noises. I couldn't understand
what was wrong with her. No one had tried to explain mental
handicap to me.

The net effect of the whole experience was that I felt I'd
been kicked out of paradise. I blamed my mother when I went
back to Esher and felt a lot of anger, I think. The memory of
that home never completely leaves me. I was on an assignment
in the South of France just a few weeks ago and, washing
my hands with cheap soap, the memory flooded back. The
combination of carbolic soap and cooking cabbage always
brings back that horrible time.

Penny Tweedie and others like her left a capital half paralysed
with apprehension beneath the summer skies. People went about
their business as usual ('London can take it!'), but without the
spirit of camaraderie and bursts of black humour that characterized
their attitude during the blitzes. Evelyn Waugh, in his deceptively
casual and throwaway manner, managed to catch the unpleasant
mood of combined languor and menace which enveloped the city
in his novel, *Unconditional Surrender*. He describes an afternoon in a
St James's club during the summer of 1944:

When Virginia's baby was ten days old and the news was
all of the Normandy landings, the dingy tranquillity which
enveloped London was disturbed. Flying bombs appeared in
the sky, unseemly little caricatures of aeroplanes, which droned
smokily over the chimney tops, suddenly fell silent, dropped
out of sight and exploded dully. Day and night they came
at frequent irregular intervals, striking at haphazard far and
near.

It was something quite other than the battle scene of the
blitz with its drama of attack and defence; its earth-shaking
concentrations of destruction and roaring furnaces; its respites
when the sirens sounded the All Clear. No enemy was risking
his own life up there. It was as impersonal as a plague, as
though the city were infected with enormous, venomous insects.
Spirits in Bellamy's, as elsewhere, had soared in the old days
when Turtle's had gone up in flames and Air Marshal Beech
had taken cover under the billiard table. Now there were glum
faces. The machines could not be heard in the bar but the tall

windows of the coffee room (cross-laced with sticking plaster) fronted St James's Street. All heads were turned towards them and a silence would fall when a motor cycle passed.

Motorcyclists were not popular in 1944 with their spluttering, back-firing machines. It was a war of acoustics and jangled nerves.

Evacuees who had returned from rural billets and had not complained when they found their homes pock-marked and the windows blasted away by the high explosive bombs of the Blitz, say the rockets affected them in the same way as having a tooth drilled without benefit of novocaine. Harry Salmon, twelve when the buzz bombs arrived, confirmed this.* Blitzed London had held no fears for him when he returned from the West Country, age nine. Facing the flying bombs three years later was different:

> Oh, I think they were the worst by far, the flying bombs, or the doodlebugs. There was something weird about them being without any pilots. It made it worse in a funny way, like you had less power over them. The nastiest thing was when you'd see them coming towards you because when they cut out and started to glide, then you knew you could be for the high jump if they were heading your way. It wasn't marvellous seeing them in back of you, or to the side of you, either, but you'd just keep hearing the putt-putt as they flew overhead and as they flew overhead, you'd pray to yourself, 'Please don't let it be me, please don't let it be me!' They were coming over East Ham way all the time, it seemed to me, night and day, day and night – never any stopping them. With the old-style piloted planes, you knew you'd have some rest in the daytime, at any rate – but not with these little horrors.

Harry Salmon thought, 'Please don't let it be me!', and wasn't alone in thinking like this. It could often seem as if the cacophonous little monsters carried personal calling cards, but so long as they putt-putted above you, you were all right. Through compressed lips many breathed a prayer, a popular mantra, that went 'keep going, keep going, keep going . . .' to the pilotless plane.

My friend, Betty Allsop, tireless charity volunteer worker and widow of Kenneth Allsop, admits that the buzz bombs inspired strange feelings of ambivalence and guilt in her. They were not

*See Chapter 4, pp. 58–9.

'noble' emotions, she told me, smiling. She was about twenty-two when she and her younger sister, Pat, were living in a house in Crouch End, North London, after her own South Thameside home had been flattened in the Blitz of 1941. Her sister, Pat, ten years younger than she, had been evacuated, and had returned to London like so many others. Betty says she remembers little of Pat's evacuation experience except that her sister complained, on her return, that her foster-parents had kept her from eating any butter while plastering it on their own pieces of bread. Many years later Pat admitted she had concocted this story to harrow her mother and family. Blitz victims, they hadn't worried overmuch about Pat's butter deprivation – or her myth about it – but had let her embroider the facts without comment. At Crouch End, Betty was happy to have her sister's company, especially in bed at night when the flying bombs went over:

> Pat and I slept on a mattress on the ground floor and I can remember when we'd hear the buzz bombs coming over, I'd bury my head in the pillow and pray to God that they would keep going. Then I'd open my eyes when one did pass over and ask myself, 'Why am I praying? I'm not religious . . .' and feel troubled by this lapse. Then I'd make myself feel even guiltier by reminding myself that in praying that the bomb would not drop on *me*, I was actually seeking the death of someone else! So I ended up lying on my pillow churning over quite a few of my lapsed principles. First of all, why was I, an agnostic, praying to God for my survival? And, secondly, what was so religious about wishing death on another person? How very un-Christian, I, a non-believer, was being! It was all pretty confusing.

Some other Londoners who lived through the doodlebug scourge were less philosophical, less soul-searching and perhaps, therefore, somewhat more cavalier about life. Such a one was Tom Scott, now sixty-nine, a West End accountant who was in the Army in 1944 and billeted in Gloucester Place. At twenty-four, he had been having a fairly pleasant war, escorting his attractive wife-to-be, Phyllis, around, and in off-duty periods sitting out the night-time blitzes of the early 40s in jovial West End pubs (the West End got off more lightly than other areas of London as far as heavy, high explosive bombardment was concerned, he points out). All in all, he says he wasn't consciously frightened, even of the doodlebugs, but his stomach, like some separate entity, responded dramatically to their passage overhead:

> I never liked the wail of sirens during the bombings of '40 and '41 and I would always listen with one ear to other people talking in the pubs and the other to the sirens and sound of gunfire. But then the V-1s came and they were more terrifying in a way. When they hit the ground, they made an awful wallop and then you'd keep an ear cocked for the sound of splintering glass. The sequence was always like that – first 'bang, wallop', then the shattered glass sound. Phyllis believes that we weren't really frightened. Sitting in the pub, we'd just go on chatting and drinking. And consciously, I wasn't. I probably appeared rather blasé. But my stomach felt otherwise. If it sank during the early bombings of the 40s, it did a real flip-flop with the buzz bombs.

Dame Josephine Barnes continued delivering babies in near impossible conditions in London in 1944.* Her own baby, Penelope, six months old, was being tended during the day by her mother at home in Barnet. Observing the rockets, Dame Josephine decided that she had to take action. She explained to me:

> I was standing by a window one night at our house high on a hill in Barnet and saw the glow of a flying bomb pass right in front of us – or so it seemed. I decided right then and there that I wouldn't endanger Penelope's life and that I had to send her out of London. At six months, she seemed awfully young to be evacuated but it had to be. I sent her to my mother-in-law's in Letchworth, Hertfordshire, and she was there for three months. In the end, I brought her back because I didn't particularly care for the way her grandmother was caring for her. She was giving Penelope things to quiet her teething pains which I thought were all wrong. It wasn't a very nice time for a young mother with a child.

The flying bombs episode was a terrifying time for the civilian population, as one can see. But they came through it bravely. Its brevity helped enormously: like an Italian February, the period had been 'corto e amaro' – short and bitter. It produced bad memories – fear of staccato noises, even of silence – and flip-flopping stomachs.

*See Chapter 7, p. 112.

But in long-range psychological terms, the episode doesn't seem to have etched itself indelibly upon many psyches or to have effected large-scale character changes. Apparently, only the evacuations of a much longer duration did that.

9

Effects of Evacuation

Memory and repression can dovetail strangely and some former evacuees say that they have only recently begun to analyse what must have been a traumatic experience of uprooting. Sometimes the trauma manifests itself merely in a curious behavioural quirk, but, with hindsight, mature evacuees now realize it was originally forged in the heat of the evacuation experience itself.

Lallie Didham, for instance, the London evacuee who became the shy, precocious toast of Manhattan night-clubs at the age of fifteen, tells of one legacy of her abrupt transplanting as a child:

> I'm a hoarder now, as I lost so many things when we left England. Today, I'm still afraid of losing things. We packed in such a hurry when we were evacuated and I was forced to leave many things which were precious to me so that it's turned me into a real magpie in middle age. I will never forget how we had to live on charity in America and I suppose I must have felt a bit put down by this as a teenager, particularly remembering what lovely possessions I had to leave behind.

As a character change created by an outside circumstance, Lallie's hoarding and 'magpie complex' is intriguing, but still a reasonably superficial effect. By contrast, one of the most disturbing effects of evacuation was to make a child find, upon return to his own home, that this home was somehow wanting. This happened when children were evacuated to grander residences than their own. It also, of course, occurred when their evacuation experience had been happy, or they had been a little spoiled while there. Naturally, this didn't always happen. Harry Salmon, the Leyton off-licence manager, returned from a fine country manor to his 'two-up, two-down' terraced house in East Ham and was thrilled to be home, even though it was not only far more humble than the country mansion he'd left, but bomb-damaged, too. But sometimes the return home to a meaner life style put a child into near shock, causing him to find his own home despicable and then to feel a little ashamed of this emotion.

Stan Clater, fifty-four, a retired merchant-navy captain, resident in Hull and now a part-time teacher of nautical studies, was sent to a friend of his maternal grandmother's during the worst of the bombing in 1940–1. Hull was blitzed in May 1941, but had previously been relatively peaceful. The May raids made up for this, mirroring the savagery of Coventry. Out of a population of 330,000 people, 40,000 were rendered homeless and 1000 were killed. How fortunate it was for eight-year-old Stan that his grandmother had privately taken it upon herself to send him away to a large farmhouse. He stayed with an elderly couple in a small Lincolnshire village just across the estuary from Hull. They were quite affluent and lived in a house filled with books. Under their tutelage he devoured the works of Jack London and Charles Dickens.

Stan enjoyed being with them, but found it odd that they wanted to appear to be his 'adoptive' parents and not his foster-parents. He was made to assume their surname. They were very attentive to him, coached him in his reading and, when he wasn't being a bookworm in their home, he cycled over to the nearby US Air Force base where American airmen showered him with chewing gum, sweets and Captain Marvell comics with what became known in wartime as the customary Yankee generosity. Stan had a good war, and wasn't prepared for the shock awaiting him when he returned.

My first feeling on coming home was claustrophobia. I was used to space – a large room of my own, stairs wide enough for two people to pass on with shallow steps and a landing half-way up big enough to hold a fair-sized table. I came back to a tiny terraced house and the first thing I saw when the front door was opened were the stairs. I had never imagined that such appalling, narrow, steep stairs could exist.

They were a continuation of the narrow, dark passageway from the front door. Two doors in this passage opened into the two rooms which made up the ground floor. The front room was the equivalent of the Victorian parlour and was never used. The back room – smaller than my previous personal room – had a fireplace and was kitchen, dining room, living room and somehow bathroom for two adults and five children. We were typical of the rest of the street. Our house was one of a block of four. These four dwellings housed a total of twenty-one children, eight parents and a couple of grandparents to boot.

It was hate at first sight. I let it be known loudly and persistently that I wanted to go back to my 'real home'.

Stan's parents seem to have handled his hurtful behaviour very understandingly. They let him go back to visit his foster-parents regularly and before long, the charms of Hull lured him back: 'going on board trawlers, riding on buses, swimming at the baths, pilfering from Woolworth's, having lots of kids to play with, exploring bombed buildings, and so on . . .', as he puts it. Later he fell for the beautiful girl next door, Valerie, and his nostalgia for Lincolnshire all but disappeared from his mind.

That Stan didn't become totally alienated from his background was a tribute to his parents' delicate handling. The realization that he lived in a 'mean street' and that his parents' lives were compressed and humble, materially speaking, hit him and threw him temporarily off balance. Fortunately, his experience as an evacuee didn't, however, make him 'look down' on his mother and father (he is a devoted son today, regularly visiting his ageing parents).

But many poor evacuees did acquire an abiding taste for the good life; once having encountered it they were loath to give it up on returning home. Two 'showbiz' personalities, Justin de Villeneuve and Michael Caine, both Cockney boys from working-class families, have spoken of the rich tastes they acquired in the manorial homes to which they were sent, as I mentioned in Chapter 2.

Justin de Villeneuve, who played Pygmalion to Twiggy's Galatea in the 1960s, was evacuated from London, age five, as the flying bombs spluttered overhead in 1944. Born Nigel Davies and living in the East End, he was taken with his adored mother, Kitty, to J. B. Priestley's glamorous, Shropshire country manor house, where he learned to enjoy 'posh' things, a taste he has never relinquished. His memories, both visual and olfactory, of his life at the home of the famous writer and wartime radio commentator are potent. He remembers eating with silver cutlery and inhaling the heady aroma of roses.

He lives, unsurprisingly, in Chelsea, where he runs a tailoring business. He is twice divorced and a father of three daughters – his youngest, age eight, is the breathy voice who has made the recorded message on his answering machine. He retains little of his origins, except perhaps a liking for slang (he is liable to sign-off a telephone conversation with 'hasta la pasta', for example). Talking with him is to find yourself trotting conversationally through 'designer' land. We spoke in April 1988, before he went to the Italian Grand Prix as a commissioned photographer (taking his Rolliflex); he was not sure what he was going to wear but it might be soft, casual jogger gear (Yamamoto) . . . Amiable, soft-voiced, busy and talented (he has written a witty autobiography, *An Affectionate Punch*), he confirms that his Shropshire days changed him for life:

> It did affect my taste for good things in life later on, no question. I learned to speak posh in Shropshire. I'm working on a musical film about the evacuation right now and one of the lead songs is called *I've Seen a Better Way*. I think that says it all.

J. B. Priestley was remote but kind. He would always dine with the evacuees he housed and he gave them lovely parties – Justin remembers a Hallowe'en celebration in particular. The author had a self-contained flat on the top floor of his manor and otherwise was not much present. 'But I remember one time when he appeared, he played a funny game pulling faces. He loved doing this. If you laughed you were out,' Justin relates.

Michael Caine admits he was marked forever by the enviable life style he enjoyed at the home of a country squire during evacuation: he did not want to *evict* the squire, he told Ian Jack of the *Observer* magazine in a recent profile, but wanted to *become* the squire, metaphorically speaking. And he has, in a way. As he is quoted as saying: 'Today I have the squire's house in my village on the Thames. I mean, it isn't *actually* the squire's house, but if you look at the psychology of me, that's what I have.'

Returning to 'Edenholme', the ridiculously grand name for his family's modest bungalow in Southampton, writer Anthony Bailey was as bereft as Stan Clater in Hull. His home for several years, as an English evacuee in America had been a vast, luxurious, suburban edifice in Dayton, Ohio as I stated previously.* Going home was like entering the wide end of a telescope and travelling in reverse.

> The symmetry of the house was visible once one was through the gate, the front door smack in the middle between the

*See Chapter 7, p. 129.

windows and door giving the impression, as with a low fore-
head, of constrained development. The front door opened onto
a narrow corridor: hemp doormat at one's feet; round brass
casing of a clockwork-operated doorbell between the letter-box
and a frosted glass panel in the top fifth of the door that cast
a pale light like that coming from the similar panel in an
interior door at the other end of the corridor. Passing along it,
I could almost touch the wall on each side by sticking my
elbows out.

Discomfiture with smaller houses; shock at tiny parents. Helen
Cuthbert, who had such a glorious time as an evacuee in Australia
(as recounted in Chapter 7) recalls her especially jarring discovery
in *The Evacuees*: 'At Southampton we were met by our parents. It
was a wonderful reunion, although I can remember thinking and
remarking how "wee" my father was . . .'
Patriotic British parents and schoolchildren who came to greet
the long-awaited evacuees thought they must be ecstatic to be back
in 'England's green and pleasant land'. Well, this wasn't always
the case as the then fifteen-year-old Helen Cuthbert goes on to
reveal:

> . . . people . . . would ask ridiculous questions such as, 'You
> must be pleased to be home – but which country do you like
> best, the United Kingdom or Australia.' Of course I would say
> here, but I hoped to return there.
>
> My parents, when we speak of this time, very generously say
> that they remember no difficulties, but I remember on one
> occasion when I had been unspeakably difficult, my Mother
> saying, 'Oh, well, we'll try it for a year, and if you are still
> unsettled, then you can return.' What it must have cost her to
> say that: having just got back a daughter after five years'
> absence!

The significant thing about Helen's answers to those who asked
her which country she liked best, I believe, is that she felt she had
to tell a lie and say 'England', though at first she didn't mean it.
To be an evacuee was a contorted business: first learning to adjust
to one strange place, then adjusting so well you come to loathe the
place you left when you return to it. The evacuee was a veritable
India rubber ball.
Learning to adapt to totally new circumstances is a sophisticated

task and one which exerts its toll on a young child. One of the qualities which sometimes gets lost in the exercise is honesty or, at least, the child can acquire a creeping case of hypocrisy, a tendency to bend the truth in order to please. Helen told everyone she preferred England to Australia upon her return to Britain five years later because, though it was untrue, it was what she thought her family and friends expected her to say, and it made life easier to respond accordingly. The trouble about being forced into a chameleon-like existence is that a child can become almost too good at changing coloration and saying things to please.

Gloria Cigman, an eleven-year-old Jewish girl from Cardiff, found herself in a farming village called Gilmorton, in the Midlands, between Rugby and Leicester, and tried to roll with all the punches this experience meted out to her, even pretending she enjoyed seeing pigs slaughtered for very porcine repasts. As she writes in *The Evacuees*:

> . . . I find that one aspect of it all emerges very powerfully. This is a kind of chameleonism that those of us who were successful evacuees cultivated. (By successful, I mean those of us who were happy and who felt accepted most of the time.) This faculty made it possible to sense what would please, what would make us acceptable, what would not alienate or offend, what would not violate the way of living into which we had been transplanted, or, by being different, imply criticism. We were tactful and appreciative. We ate what we were given and enjoyed it, we did not just pretend to enjoy it. I learned to eat with relish every single part of a pig, despite my upbringing which not only excluded all pig-derived food, but regarded the eating of it as a violation of a God-given law. My Gilmorton family would nurture a pig to gross proportions, then send it down the road for slaughter . . . then render every single part of that pig edible: pork, bacon, ham, trotters, head, tail. I loved it all.

Gloria Cigman ate the pig in an almost masochistic way, like a Christian missionary exulting in a cannibal feast in the bush.

Evacuees could almost taste the humility of *having* to adapt and come to enjoy it. But they doubtless lost something in the effort of refining their own hypocritical act. Tom Wolfe, the author, is fond of saying that 'a liberal is a conservative who has been arrested' (a phrase oft-repeated in his latest success, *The Bonfire of the Vanities*), and bearing the same kind of thinking in mind you could say that the well-adjusted evacuee child was the one who made evacuation work for him. For if a trauma is needed to reshape one's stance or alter one's convictions, then the evacuation process, like an unexpected arrest, did this admirably well. But for a child to have to remodel his or her beliefs or entire personality so drastically, for the sake of survival, must mean the loss of something else – innocence.

Jonathan Miller, who described watching his father talking to a Welsh farmer on a hazy but ominous summer's day (see pp. 102–103), says that all the travelling about he and his family did to evade bombs has probably left him with a lasting passion to stay in the same place. As he told me:

I suppose travelling from one place to another and having no stable home when I was seven and eight has had its lasting effect. My wife is sure that it has. I do tend to cleave to my home. I've been here in my Northwest London home for twenty years. I travel around a great deal but I've always liked the idea of returning to a familiar base.

But I don't think you could say that the iron entered my soul in any way. It was a comfortable evacuation. We followed our father around. It wasn't self-consciously an evacuation for us. It was more that my father and mother wanted to get the family beyond the reach of the bombs. Father was fortunate in being too old to be posted abroad so we saw him a lot. He was here with the War Office making a statistical analysis of war recruits. There was a lot of moving around for us, all the same. During the Phoney War of 1939, we went to South Wales and stayed at our nanny's house in Monmouthshire near Tintern Abbey. Later on, during the flying bombs episode, Mother picked us up again and took us to North Wales. The only real terror I can recall was in 1944 when I was ten with the so-called doodlebugs. We lived twenty miles north of London in Watford and so were more or less out of their over-fly space but I was terrified of the siren warnings. They were prolonged warnings, going on for six hours at a time. There was no off and on wailing as you had during the earlier blitzes. Also, there was that terrible phrase used by the War Office to tell us about them – 'pilotless planes'. It was as if someone told you 'Dracula's bats are here . . .'

I do go back to Wales as often as I can. I've developed a
passion for the long, hot heat of summers. I love hot valleys,
supernatural quiet, the warm woodlands and pregnant silence,
the sense of expectancy. It's been cleared now of any sense of
actual physical dread.

Some psychiatrists of the day were implacably opposed to the
evacuation scheme and reiterate their antipathy today. One such
is the British expert on separation anxiety, John Bowlby, sometimes
considered a fuddy-duddy for preaching against the separation of
mother and child in the first two years of childhood (a dictum
which, of course, condemns the working mother who goes back to
work during her child's first two years of life), but who is revered
by child development specialists, all the same. At eighty, he still
researches and teaches at the Tavistock Clinic in London, although
he retired as a consultant psychiatrist there in the early 1970s. His
conviction, that mothering should be a continuous process from the
child's early infancy, only to be broken at the age of two and a half,
and then only in short spells when the child attends a pre-school or
nursery, has remained unshaken for half a century. The severance
of what he sees as the crucial mother-child link during evacuation
alarmed him in 1939. As a young man he voiced his reservations
to the Ministry of Health when it formulated the evacuation policy,
but was ignored. He told *Sunday Times* reporter Helen Mason, in a
piece entitled 'Are Mothers Necessary?' (13 December 1987):

> Evacuation was a bad mistake and it was the child guidance
> people who had to pick up the pieces. The result was the
> writing into the education bill of 1944, the Butler Act, that
> there be 'a child guidance service throughout the country'.

The late Anna Freud, the renowned child analyst, also supported
the view that long-term separation from a beloved parent is detri-
mental to a child's emotional growth (see Chap. 3). She was
convinced that a child benefited from having a minimum of 'dis-
continuity' with the sole 'psychological' parent (who needn't always
be the blood parent but the one who was consistently there; the
'sole' parent could, of course, in a minority of cases be the father).
The best chance for a child's healthy psychological growth, in her
view, was for it to be with the adult who was 'available on an
uninterrupted day-to-day basis'.

Anna Freud's belief that a child should remain with one 'psychological' parent appeared in one of the last studies she wrote (1973); her subject was divorce, the child and legal custody (by inference, split or shared custody, in her view, was the least healthy solution). Curiously enough, she had arrived at this controversial conviction late in life as a result of her many years spent analysing children, and also her study of the effects of evacuation and parental loss on pre-school-aged children. She and her co-worker, Dorothy Burlingham, who helped enlighten people about 'enuresis', directed a residential nursery near Chelmsford, Essex, from December 1940 to the end of February 1942. The pair supervised the well-being of 138 infants and pre-schoolers; 103 were residents of the nurseries, 35 non-residents. The experience of caring for over a year for these children, who had lost one or both parents in the war, led them to conclude that the separation of a child from his or her parent or parents was far more distressing to them than the bombs from which they were being protected.

Anna Freud noted that the young children behaved in a bereaved way, regressing to infantile behaviour such as bedwetting, thumbsucking, compulsive eating, aggressive and destructive attitudes towards both animate and inanimate objects, rocking, hair-chewing, muteness and masturbating. Others monotonously repeated the word which recalled their lost mothers, such as seventeen-month-old Christine who said: 'Mum, mum, mum, mum,' continually in a deep voice for three days.

Bereavement in the young child caused it to 'clam-up' alarmingly, too, as Anna Freud noted:

> The children who had lost their fathers in air raids never mentioned anything of their experience for many months . . . After a year, two of them at least told the complete story with no details left out . . . The child begins to talk about the incident when the feelings which were aroused by it have been dealt with in some other manner.

To this heart-rending picture of child mourning and repression, Anna Freud gave some light. As she said, speech helped a child to air its disturbed feelings and the older child, at least, was better able to cope with his grief: 'Towards the age of five, this mental understanding already helps in lessening the shock.'

It is just as well to remember that Anna Freud was dealing with full or partial orphans and while the average evacuee might have experienced some feelings of grief when separated from his or her parents (as did Margaret Hanton, who was sent to Canada, and no doubt many others like her), most were able, dimly at least, to understand *why* this separation had occurred, so that reason helped the over-fives to accept enforced separation.

In any case, the experts disagree about the effect of evacuation on children. Dame Josephine Barnes, a contemporary of Dr Bowlby's, firmly told me that the switch from town to country probably benefited the evacuees:

> The idea that the only one who should look after the child is the mother is nonsense. Being sent away from your home could be beneficial. The towns were terribly smoky and dangerous in the 40s and going away to cleaner air definitely improved children's health. In some cases, children were sent to a farm where there were two parents, whereas the child might have only had one in town, especially during the war when the men were away fighting. So a child in this case would have had a substitute father for the duration. It taught a child independence. And of course, it also taught children how the other half lived – in this case, rural people – which was a good thing. It wasn't always a success but then every real family is not a success, either.

What I have observed personally from my interviews with evacuees is that many of them have repressed the unhappier aspects of their evacuation experience. While consciously they would tell themselves, 'Mum sent me away to keep me safe', unconsciously they often felt their departure unjust.

Kathy Tuffin (see pp. 50–1) started to cry recently when telling her daughter of how wretchedly thirsty she'd been on her train ride from London to the North. She had been offered milky tea instead of water at the reception centre, and this seemed intolerable to her at the time – worse than leaving her beloved home, loving grandparents and tearful mother – although probably her outrage served to focus all the horrors she had endured on one simple grievance – thirst. She had felt like Alice when offered a dry biscuit from the Red Queen after running a race in the summer heat. Outraged! What amazed her, she says now, is that she didn't cry then but was stolid, demanding 'water' like a trade unionist his rights. Nearly fifty years later, she cried for the pain and humiliation she had experienced, and repressed, as a seven-year-old child.

Sometimes, tucking a bad memory away for the sake of survival means it transforms itself into a recurrent dream that emerges whenever one is anxious about daily events. I have an idea that the mental eye of the evacuee was wide open, like a camera lens about to snap a picture, especially when the experience was new and fresh. Eva Figes writes of the image imprinted on her schoolgirl psyche when she flew off from Tempelhof, Germany, in 1938, and left her adored grandparents behind (see pp. 99–100). She recounts her nightmare in *Little Eden: A Child at War*: 'For years, I was to take off, in a recurring dream, leaving them all behind, under that dark menacing sky . . .'

For my own part, huge waves wash my dream-life when times get rough. My mother and I were evacuated from Mukden, Manchuria in November 1940, when I was eleven. (President Roosevelt ordered women and children out of Asia in November 1940, presciently, as it happened, since the Japanese attack on the US Fleet at Pearl Harbor on 7 December 1941 took place only thirteen months later.) The US liner, the S.S. *Mariposa*, took us uneventfully across the Pacific, but a few days outside San Francisco we ran into a typhoon. The hundred-foot-high waves on each side of the ship formed ominous, grey, cascading hills of water. My mother, a stunning thirty-nine year old dressed in dashing culottes, the chic garb of the day, sat on the floor near the cabin door holding a huge glass filled with dark whisky and ice cubes, and listened to them clink from side to side. I huddled close, trying to look upon this tempest as a lucky adventure (it wasn't – seventy-five people were injured in the storm). Today, as a mature woman, whenever I am troubled, I have my 'wave' dream; I see them mounting, lapping and engulfing me on a beach or from a shore approaching my house. For years, close friends told me this is a typical Jungian image of the collective unconscious – 'waves are breasts . . . you know, the feminine image or symbol . . . you're an earth mother dreaming about the ultimate woman, etc., etc.' What rubbish; it is nothing of the sort. My psychic camera snapped an alarming sight that took place in frightening times, and years later the beautiful, scary waves resurfaced from the depths of my unconscious as a reminder of personal danger.

Being an evacuee may be uncomfortable but it doesn't hurt actively so presumably children can take it. But can they? To judge

from the evacuees I've met, and from my own experience, I'd say
it can be a more disturbing event than it appears from the outside
(boredom often mars the faces of the evacuees pictured in this book,
but rarely outright fear or horror, and sometimes, of course, their
faces register pure glee). The word evacuation is and was bother-
some. The painter, John Furse, found himself turning it around and
around in his seven-year-old mind when he was evacuated from
London to Devon in 1939, an etymological pursuit he detailed in
The Evacuees:

> I was evacuated: I looked up the meaning of the word and it
> all seemed to fit. The word means, so it said –
>
> > evacuate, v.t. (–uable) empty.
> > (stomach, etc.); ('esp. of troops')
> > withdraw from (place);
> > discharge (excrement, etc.)
> > evacuation, n. (vacuum).
>
> It all fits, the withdrawing, the emptiness, the troops, the
> vacuum – above all the vacuum. I was evacuated: I won't
> comment on the excrement.

The indignity of the role was not lessened by knowing the meaning
of the word.

The evacuees were often jeered at in towns, called 'vaccies',
'vacs', 'skinnies' (in Wales, it seems, because they looked so much
thinner than rural children) and avoided. Of necessity, they were
thrown in upon themselves or forced to isolate themselves in school
groups. In America, the term was often allied in the host country's
mind with poverty (and genuinely so – the CORB children received
six shillings a week – a sum which after four years and much growth,
from young child to gangling teenager, hardly paid for his or her
morning cornflakes). The American-based evacuees frequently said
they felt like 'poor relations' or 'poor cousins'; or that they were
living 'on charity'. Author Diana Phipps said she learned about
making interiors attractive, cheaply, as an adolescent 'emigrant' to
America after a rather more glamorous childhood in a Czechoslo-
vakian castle from which she was evacuated during the wartime
ravages of the 40s, first as a result of German occupation and then
of a Communist take-over. She found herself in what she describes as
an 'ugly and very small' American house with, a prized possession, a

tiny room of her own. She recalls vividly in her witty 'how-to-do' book, *Affordable Splendour*, that all these 'zingy' ideas on being imaginatively poor occurred to her as she stretched gingham over grocery cardboard boxes in this modest evacuee abode, an impoverished European aristocrat with more dash than cash.

Many, like Diana Phipps, refused to go under. Lallie Didham, by dint of charm and high spirits, became the somewhat reluctant belle of Manhattan night clubs, and Margaret Hanton stunned them in Toronto with her academic prowess. Many evacuees, reluctant to face being put down, either as a 'poor cousin' or a stranger, became high-flyers, even entrepreneurial wizards.

In literature, the evacuee is presented as the rank outsider. Jeremy Seabrook, in his book, *Mother and Son*, said he viewed the visiting evacuees with awe: 'they threatened chaos and disorder . . . I envied his [an evacuee's] freedom . . .'

They are a group apart, to whom strange things have already happened and others are anticipated. I don't think it is a coincidence that the four young people – Peter, Susan, Edmund and Lucy – in *The Lion, the Witch and the Wardrobe*, the children's fable by C. S. Lewis were evacuees or, in Lewis's words, 'sent away from London during the war because of the air-raids'. The strange old house they go to ('ten miles from the nearest railway station and two miles from the nearest post office', run by four servants and a very old man with shaggy white hair) was made for magic. It seems only logical that Lucy should step through the back of a wardrobe and find crunchy snow, a faun and pine forests. Think how an evacuee from a slum in Tottenham must have felt about the cloisters at King's College, Cambridge! To be transported from one environment to another in a moment is the essence of magic, and evacuees experienced it every day.

But as magical and pleasant an experience as evacuation could be, it was, as we have seen, also bewildering and frequently humiliating to young evacuees. Government spokesmen bewailed the children's propensity to have head-lice and wet their beds; foster-parents often made no attempt to disguise their shock at the way they were 'sewn into their rags'. One disturbing aspect of being an evacuee was a feeling of schizophrenia, as evidenced in the case of the young teenager in Elizabeth Ogg's article on the 'Blitz Children', who held on to her British accent in America, but returned home and became violently American, waving the Stars and Stripes for years. Other young evacuees who didn't like the

feeling of being cut in two, decided to opt for the colours and habits
of the host nation altogether.

Catherine Robinson, a 51-year-old school-teacher living in Bel-
mont, Mass., outside Boston, was a three-year-old evacuee from
Dunwich, Suffolk in 1940. Her first memory of the sea trip across
the Atlantic in the company of her mother was that she was not
able to see her brother from her bunk and found this unsettling.
Her family tell her now how difficult she was to begin with, missing
her mother, who returned to England. But eventually, she moved
in with Madeleine Crawford, an inspirational science teacher living
in Needham, Mass., and she learned to love her 'Aunt', as she still
thinks of her today:

> I made it as hard on my mother as an eight year old can when
> I returned to England five years later. I kept complaining, 'I
> want to go back to Aunt Madeleine.' I suppose it was only
> natural. I had been a virtual only child with her as my brother
> returned to England before me.

Later on she did return to go to college at Pine Manor, then in
Wellesley, Mass. It was a natural and happy move as Madeleine
Crawford had joined the science staff in 1947; Catherine could be
with her favourite 'Aunt' again. Her older sister and brother remained in England and she visits them on occasion. But it is
obvious that she feels wholly American, happy with her college-age,
'typically' American children and her lawyer husband:

> I love to visit England and my children have all been over at
> least three times each. But I am 100 per cent American and
> am a citizen. I do not believe one should live in a country made
> up of emigrants unless you become a citizen. Also, I could not
> be a different nationality from my children. So I guess you
> could say I do not miss England, but I do respect the English
> in many ways.
>
> I suspect that a lot of what I believe is because of my
> background. I know what happened to me as a child has had
> an effect on the way I am today. I keep in very close touch
> with my children when they are away and encourage them to
> do the same among themselves, in part, because I felt cut off
> from my siblings. I have tried to do things as a family far more
> than my [own] family did. We travel together, visit among the
> colleges that the children attend and encourage each child to

take an interest in his or her siblings. I think my mother acted as a clearing house for our communications between siblings. I want the children to develop their own relationships with each other.

I think I always wanted to live in one place, to have friends who grew up with me. I was not good at making lasting friendships as a teenager because I had never had friendships that were allowed to last. I have many acquaintances but no 'best' friends left from my school or college days.

I think it is fair to say that Madeleine has had the most influence on me with the exception of my husband. I think the years from eight to eighteen in England were not really very happy years as I never let myself forget America. I never developed an adult relationship with my parents on visits home as a grown-up. I let them dictate what I did. This past summer I returned to England for the first time since their death seven years ago. For the first time, I felt in control. My oldest daughter was also there – she's twenty-five and married – and we had a wonderful time visiting family and friends.

Obviously, Catherine Robinson held the belief that to make a good omelette, you have to break eggs. Tenaciously, she kept the idea of America in her mind for ten years, as a growing child and adolescent, and returned there for good as a young adult at eighteen. A sensitive, intelligent woman, she perceives rooting herself in America as an act of free will, a quality she treasures, and she also realizes that it has something to do with 'control'. Her own parents were 'over-controlling'; her Aunt Madeleine urged her to think for herself. I think it is fair to say that in the most extreme of cases (and there were innumerable children like Catherine who embraced the host country forever), a flaw in the parent-child relationship was also a contributing factor in the child's decision to stay abroad. The combination of an early evacuation, youthful bonding to a lovable surrogate parent, a long stay abroad and domineering natural parents all added up, in Catherine's case, to a joyful and totally voluntary expatriation.

Certainly, Catherine Robinson's clear-cut and definite choice has meant a happier outcome for her compared to those who were left feeling forever divided by immersion in two different cultures and the inability to bestow full allegiance on one or the other. Catherine, blessedly, does not, like so many Californian 'Brits' living in the

American sunshine, moan endlessly about missing 'the river mists' or 'bangers and mash' or 'Marmite'. In her separation from her native land, she was her own surgeon and the cut was clean.

Catherine Robinson's remarks about not being able to make lasting friendships – for fear, perhaps, of losing them? – is more true of the effects on overseas evacuees than on the ones who moved about inside Britain. In fact, Hilary Granger says that the other evacuees, who dropped anchor with her at Billesdon Manor School during the war, have become a virtual sisterhood, meeting annually like college or university alumnae. Robin Mitchell looks back on his evacuee days as a charmed period, a lost boyhood he likes to return to tap into each year, an antidote to the pressures of his work life. Others could not be dragged to those former sites; Mary Baxter loves the West Country, for example, but always by-passes North Devon, her billeting ground.

The effect of early disruption was most far-reaching, I found, in the evacuees' attitudes to their own children. It was rare to find a former evacuee who had sent his or her children to boarding school, for example, and many said they had to struggle to sever ties though they knew this exercise to be necessary for the growth of healthy independence in their own children. Lallie Didham found the departure of her youngest child from her Kenyan home similar to a bereavement; I, too, remember going into temporary decline when my son decided to seek his fortune in America, though it is my country. Ex-evacuees don't like bidding their children goodbye and have to struggle hard against being over-protective. Kathy Tuffin says she didn't even feel comfortable when her children went on brief summer holidays abroad. There is, altogether, a lot of teeth-gritting among graduates of the evacuation experience where their children are concerned. In psychiatric terms, many adult evacuees have 'internalized' their experience; they battened down the hatches of their grief and separation anxiety at the time of being evacuated, but every time they are parted from a child, the experience is relived, making the parting doubly painful.

Margaret Hanton says that the experience of being separated for over five years from her mother in Canada had the effect of making her very indecisive in later life. She can make cast-iron decisions over important matters, but simpler ones wrack her soul. Purchasing any large item throws her into turmoil: when buying a car, deciding on the make hurls her into a confusion which far outweighs whatever is at stake. Again, I can identify with her. I put down four deposits and had three surveys done on different flats before moving into my present one. The exigencies of daily life – buying cars, moving house – make us relive feelings of early disruption with double intensity. We are easily fragmented though the re-forming process is quick; no one is apt to suffer but ourselves. After all, don't we have to be nice and acquiescent – under penalty of what – banishment?

Pondering over evacuation, my own and hundreds of others, I have come to the conclusion that it had happier results in social and historical, even economic terms, than on the individual psyche. The legacy of the World War II evacuations totally benefited the welfare of British children born after them.

Until recently it has been usual in Western society to regard the child, not as an entity apart, but merely as an extension of the adults to whom it belongs, and often a rather irritating extension at that. In the last century, the pain of repeated confinements, and the endless child deaths that followed, had a corrosive effect on the adult's view of the child. A son or a daughter was a possession; a mere chattel. If a child was sufficiently sturdy to reach the age of five, he was considered robust enough to be treated as an adult – and this meant that he or she could work like an adult, as well. Two British social historians, Ivy Pinchbeck and Margaret Hewitt, expressed their conviction that children in pre-industrial and industrial Britain were regarded as 'little adults . . . little attempt was made to soften life for them.'

The belief in the 'sanctity of parenthood' made it very difficult to get any legislation through parliament to prevent parents from being cruel and exploitive to their children, who were sent in their thousands into wool and coal factories and up chimneys to sweep from the age of five onwards. The law enabling the prosecution of cruel parents, which the British NSPCC tried to have passed in 1889, did not enter the statute books until forty-four years later in 1933, in the form of the Children and Young Persons Act, which decreed that anyone over the age of sixteen who 'wilfully assaults, ill-treats, neglects, abandons or exposes him [a child] . . . in a manner likely to cause him unnecessary suffering', is deemed guilty of misdemeanour. In the US, children fared better and protective legislation on their behalf was passed in some states as early as 1876.

Children's health was also becoming more of a matter for State and individual medical and charitable concern. Frederick Truby King, a New Zealand paediatrician who settled in Britain, produced his child care manual, *Feeding and Care of Baby*, in 1913 and, while people may smile at the rigid feeding timetables he decreed for baby, he did save thousands of infants' lives in London's East End, for example, by teaching poor mothers about sterilizing milk and bottles. His dietary advice was sound, too. He recommended a great many protein-rich ingredients (eggs, fish and chicken) for growing children; citrus fruits for Vitamin C (oranges and grapefruit juice); and issued warnings against fatty foods, starches and follies like raw onions. He also cautioned mothers against giving tea, coffee, cider and beer to their children.

This was progress, indeed, on the dietary and medical fronts. However, judging from the reports about the evacuees' health coming out of the cities in World War II, Truby King's advice had been lost somewhere down the line. The Women's Institutes reported young children living on OXO cubes and broken biscuits; toddlers washing down cheese with beer; and mothers feeding nursing infants tinned sardines. What had happened?

The Depression of the Thirties had happened, sharply reducing all visible signs of progress amongst the poor in the inner-cities where diet and dress and hygiene were concerned. The world economic slump, which began with the Wall Street crash in 1929, had sent its shock waves over Britain. In 1932, there were nearly three million workers 'laid off'. The unemployment figures varied from region to region with the most affected areas in the North, the least affected in the Southeast; variations echoed in today's figures. Wales was the worst hit with one in three men out of work; one in four in Scotland; one in five in the Midlands and London, and the Southeast faring the best with one in eight. Some towns in the 'depressed areas' became renowned for their misery, notably the Tyneside shipbuilding town of Jarrow, enshrined in history now for its 'Jarrow March' on 5 October 1936, when unemployed workers marched to the Houses of Parliament to protest against the Means Test, some in slippers, the soles of which were nearly gone by the time they reached Westminster.

Children were so weak from malnutrition in Jarrow that they had to leave school at three o'clock in the afternoon at the latest, unable to muster the strength to continue after that, one Jarrow March survivor recalled in a memorial programme broadcast on Channel

4 in 1986. Often, tea, the main meal, was a tin of sardines. Angus Calder states:

> Life became an indignity [for the unemployed]. The street corner and the public library were the habitat of the hopeless. After unemployment insurance ran out, men fell back on 'transitional payments' or on 'public assistance', on 'the dole'. To draw the full dole, they had to prove need, and from 1934 onwards the authorities operated the infamous 'Household Means Test', whereby the earnings, savings and other assets of all members of the family were assumed to be available to support the unemployed man.

It is small wonder that the schoolchildren who turned up on the platforms of rural towns to be billeted in September 1939 arrived in such a parlous state; with dirty heads, split plimsolls on their feet, often sewn into their rags and ready to attack their soup with a knife and fork at the table.* They were the children of Britain's mass unemployed, 'the bud of the nation' reared in the depressed industrial cities of the North, the Midlands and the Northeast. The evacuation turned a national telescope on these hundreds of thousands of deprived children hitherto forgotten in the shadow of their parents' misery.

The evacuation was also a remarkable historical happening because it enabled the 'haves' to meet 'the have nots' directly. It is certainly to the credit of a compassionate nation that these ghastly conditions of poverty and neglect affecting a large section of its children were not allowed to go unchanged. As historian Richard Titmuss has said, the evacuation began 'a compulsory levelling-up of standards' and, in another passage, that it 'functioned as a disguised welfare agency'. Billeting officers reported conditions back to local councils; local councils reported to the Ministry of Health; the Ministry of Health declared that such essentials as clothing, bedding and medical treatment ought to be provided for the needy evacuees in their billets; parents on the poverty-line in the cities should be given financial relief . . . In the midst of disaster and wartime muddle, the Welfare State was born with the improvement

---

*Children from Newcastle were described by Women's Institute members as follows: 'Soup seemed to be unknown to some of the children. One mother admitted they never had soup, while two boys (ten and twelve) attempted it with a knife and fork.'

of the condition of the country's children as a prime target in its constitution. Children became, at last, a first priority.

Lord Beveridge, principal architect of the Welfare State, found in the conditions of the evacuees all the tangible human evidence he suspected existed to write his famous Report. His concern for children is clearly shown in a passage from a book on social policies written in 1944, called *Full Employment in a Free Society*: 'The worst feature of Want in Britain shortly before this war was its concentration upon children . . . Nearly half of all the working-class children in the country were born into Want.'

The evacuation scheme had had a convoluted career – started as a short-term safety measure, it became far more – the foundation stone of future child welfare policies in the post-war world. And this legacy lingers on. As I write, *The Times* reports that the present government has suffered a defeat in the House of Lords (4 March 1988) with peers calling for a clause to ensure that any review of the level of child benefit undertaken each April, take account of increases in the Retail Price Index. (Child benefit had been frozen by the Conservative government.) Lady Strange (Conservative) asserted that child benefit was of inestimable value to parents, in many cases, because, as she stressed:

> When the cost of living goes up, children's appetites do not go down and their feet do not stop growing . . . It seems essential that benefit for children should continue to go on and keep pace with the cost of living. If this were not so, it might not be a case of half a loaf but of no bread at all.

It is significant, in my opinion, that while many post-war welfare policies have been abandoned as a consequence of the 1980s new-style radicalism, those pertaining to child welfare remain stubbornly in place. And I am convinced that the evacuation scheme, cobbled together so clumsily half a century ago, is, in part, responsible. As a social experiment with far-reaching influence, it remains almost unparalleled.

The individual evacuees were unaware of the momentous changes they, as a group, had set in motion. However, the significance – personal and historical – of the end of the war provoked eloquent responses from them. Here is how fifteen-year-old Hilary Granger, the Billesdon, Leicestershire evacuee, recorded in her diary that happy day of 8 May:

VE-Day at last. We went into the village to look at the decorations. People had done their best but you could tell that they were obviously decorations left over from the Coronation. At 3 p.m. we listened to Winston Churchill broadcast the official declaration of the end of the war in Europe. His closing words were very stirring: 'Forward Britannia, onward the cause of freedom, long live the King.' We then prepared the bonfire for the evening . . . we built an enormous bonfire and all the little ones stood around it and a few village children came also and we sang songs and gave cheers for everyone and everything we could think of. At 7.30 p.m. we went to the Thanksgiving Service at Church. At 9 p.m. the King broadcast . . . he managed very well[!] After supper we made another huge bonfire which was much more effective than the first one because it was dark. The flames leapt upwards and we all went mad, we seized mouth organs, combs and anything we could find which would make a noise. Then we did the Hokey Cokey round the fire, the Chestnut Tree round the flower beds and the Lambeth Walk round the pear tree. At 10 p.m. the Nursery girls went to bed. We put the fire out and followed at 11 p.m. We woke up at just gone midnight to hear the whole village processing down the street to the accompaniment of a piano accordion. We all leant out of the window and yelled. There was a big glow in the sky from a bonfire in Skeffington and green and red rockets were going off everywhere.

Sources

Chapter One
Titmuss, Richard M., 'Problems
  of Social Policy', in *Official History
  of the Second World War*, HMSO
  and Longmans, London,
  1950.
Churchill, Winston, *The Second
  World War*, Vol. 1, 'The
  Gathering Storm', Cassell,
  London, 1948.
Johnson, B. S. (ed.), *The Evacuees*,
  Gollancz, London, 1968.
Longmate, Norman (ed.), *The Home
  Front: An Anthology of Personal
  Experiences 1938–1945*, Chatto and
  Windus, London, 1981.
Brittain, Vera, *England's Hour, An
  Autobiography 1939–1941*, Futura,
  London, 1981.
Lewis, Peter, *A People's War*,
  Methuen (a Channel 4 book),
  London, 1986.
Graves, Charles, *The Home Guard
  of Britain*, Hutchinson, London,
  1943.
Johnson, Derek E., *Exodus of
  Children*, Pennyfarthing
  Publications, Clacton-on-Sea,
  Essex, 1985.

Chapter Two
Jackson, Dr Carlton, *Who Will
  Take Our Children?*, Methuen,
  London, 1985.
Isaacs, Dr Susan (ed.), *The
  Cambridge Evacuation Survey: A
  Wartime Study in Social Welfare and
  Education*, Methuen, London,
  1941.
Titmuss, Richard M., op. cit.
Bondfield, Rt Hon. Margaret
  (ed.), *Our Towns: A Close-Up*,
  'A Study made in 1939–42 by
  the Hygiene Committee of the
  Women's Group on Public
  Welfare', Oxford University
  Press, Oxford, 1943.
*Government Evacuation Scheme, Notes
  for Billeting Officers and Voluntary
  Welfare Workers*, HMSO,
  London, 1941.
Lewis, Peter, op. cit.
Zelizer, Viviana A., *Pricing the
  Priceless Child: The Changing
  Social Value of Children*, Basic
  Books, New York, 1987.
Waugh, Evelyn, *Put Out More
  Flags*, Penguin, London,
  1983.
Kops, Bernard, *The World is a
  Wedding*, Valentine, Mitchell,
  London, 1973.
Johnson, Derek E., op. cit.
Brittain, Vera, op. cit.

Chapter Three
Churchill, Winston, *The Second World War*, Vol. II, 'Their Finest Hour', Cassell, London, 1949.
Mass Observation Archives, University of Sussex (File Reports: 151, 15B, 2189).
Isaacs, Dr Susan (ed.), op. cit.
Figes, Eva, *Little Eden: A Child at War*, Faber, London, 1978.
National Federation of Women's Institutes, *Town Children through Country Eyes: A Survey on Evacuation*, published in Dorking, Surrey, by the WI, 1940.
Freud, Anna and Burlingham, Dorothy, *Children in War-Time*, Methuen, London, 1940.
Titmuss, Richard M., op. cit.
Waller, Jane and Vaughan-Rees, Michael, *Women in Wartime: The Role of Women's Magazines 1939–1945*, Optima, London, 1987.

Chapter Four
Jackson, Dr Carlton, op. cit.
Isaacs, Dr Susan (ed.), op. cit.
Gadd, Eric Wyeth, *Hampshire Evacuees, the War Time Diary, 1939, of Eric Wyeth Gadd*, Paul Cave, Southampton, 1982.
Inglis, Brian and Grundy, Bill, *All Our Yesterdays*, (from the Granada TV series), Orbis, London, 1974.
Mass Observation Archives (File Reports: 17, 299).

Chapter Five
Bates, L. M., *The Battle of London River, 1939–1945*, Lavenham Press, Lavenham, Suffolk, 1985.
Mass Observation Archives (File Reports: 392, 412).

Calder, Angus, *The People's War*, Granada, London, 1982.
Titmuss, Richard M., op. cit.
Carey, John (ed.), *The Faber Book of Reportage*, Faber, London, 1987.
Johnson, B. S. (ed.), *The Evacuees*, Gollancz, London, 1968.
Longmate, Norman (ed.), op. cit.
Gadd, Eric Wyeth, op. cit.
Government Evacuation Scheme, Memo. Ev. 4, issued by the Ministry of Health, HMSO, London, 1939.
Illingworth, Frank, *Britain Under Shellfire*, Hutchinson, London, 1942.
Portsmouth Local History Group (WEA), *Portsmouth at War*, Buckland, 1983.
Kops, Bernard, op. cit.
Brittain, Vera, op. cit.

Chapter Six
Fitzgibbon, Constantine, *The Blitz*, Macdonald, London, 1970.
Titmuss, Richard, M., op. cit.
Read, Piers Paul, *The Free Frenchman*, The Alison Press/Secker and Warburg, London, 1986.
Figes, Eva, op. cit.
Isaacs, Dr Susan (ed.), op. cit.
Johnson, B. S. (ed.), op. cit.

Chapter Seven
Ogg, Elizabeth, 'Report on the Blitz Children We Sheltered', NY *Times* magazine, 11 November 1946.
Jackson, Dr Carlton, op. cit.
Forester, C. S., *News Letter from America*, 'The Home Front, 1942',

(statistics on Lend-Lease Supplies from US to UK in 1940) reproduced in *The Home Front: The Best of Good Housekeeping 1939–1945*, compiled by Braithwaite, B., Walsh, N., and Davies, G., Ebury Press, London, 1987.

Barker, Ralph, *The Children of the Benares*, Methuen, London, 1987.

Brittain, Vera, op. cit.

Maclean, Meta, *The Singing Ship*, Angus and Robertson, London, 1941.

Johnson, B. S. (ed.), op. cit.

Davis, Eric, 'Boy on a Raft', *Reader's Digest*, New York, January 1941 (pp. 12–14); condensed from *Liberty* magazine, 28 December 1940.

Bailey, Anthony, *England, First and Last*, Viking, New York, 1985.

Chester, Lewis, Linklater, Magnus, and May, David, *Jeremy Thorpe: A Secret Life*, Deutsch, London, 1979.

Chapter Eight

Mack, Joanna and Humphries, Steven, *London at War: The Making of Modern London 1939–1945*, Sidgwick & Jackson (with London Weekend television), London, 1985.

Tedder, J. M., *With Prejudice*, Cassell, London, 1960.

Terraine, John, *The Right of the Line*, Hodder and Stoughton, London, 1985.

Nixon, Barbara, *Raiders Overhead*, Scolar/Gulliver, London, revised and enlarged edition, 1980.

Waugh, Evelyn, *Unconditional Surrender*, Chapman and Hall, London, 1961.

Chapter Nine

Villeneuve, Justin de, *An Affectionate Punch*, Sidgwick & Jackson, London, 1986.

Bailey, Anthony, op. cit.

Johnson, B. S. (ed.), op. cit.

Bowlby, John, *Loss, Sadness and Depression*, final volume of the 'Attachment and Loss' series, Hogarth Press, London, 1980.

Freud, Anna and Burlingham, Dorothy, op. cit.

Freud, Anna, Goldstein, Joseph, and Solnit, Albert J., *Beyond the Best Interests of the Child*, The Free Press, New York and London, 1973.

Figes, Eva, op. cit.

Phipps, Diana, *Affordable Splendour*, Weidenfeld and Nicolson, London, 1984.

Seabrook, Jeremy, *Mother and Son*, Gollancz, London, 1979.

Lewis, C. S., *The Lion, the Witch and the Wardrobe*, Puffin, London, 1959.

Ogg, Elizabeth, op. cit.

Pinchbeck, Ivy and Hewitt, Margaret, *Children in English Society*, Vol. II, Routledge & Kegan Paul, London, 1973.

King, Frederick Truby, *Feeding and Care of Baby*, Oxford University Press, London, 1913.

Calder, Angus, op. cit.

National Federation of Women's Institutes, op. cit.

Titmuss, Richard M., op. cit.

Beveridge, W. H., *Full Employment in a Free Society*, Allen & Unwin, London, 1944.

Index